FACING EAST

Essays on
Germany, the Balkans, and Russia
in the Twentieth Century

SIR LEWIS NAMIER

HARPER TORCHBOOKS
The Academy Library
Harper & Row, Publishers, New York

FACING EAST

This book was originally published in 1947 by Hamish Hamilton, Ltd., London, and is here reprinted by arrangement. The first chapter of the original edition, "The First Mountebank Dictator," is omitted in the Torchbook edition, since this material appears as Chapter VII of *Vanished Supremacies* (TB/1088).

First HARPER TORCHBOOK edition published 1966 by Harper & Row, Publishers, Incorporated, 49 East 33rd Street, New York, N.Y. 10016.

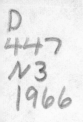

CONTENTS

ACKNOWLEDGMENTS

I have to thank the editors of *The Times*, *The Times Literary Supplement*, *The Manchester Guardian*, *Time and Tide*, *The Nineteenth Century and After*, and *The New Judaea* for permission to reprint articles that appeared in their pages.

L. B. N.

London, 10 *January* 1947

1

THE COURSE OF GERMAN HISTORY

AT THIS time we no longer take naïve pride in the scientific advance or in the technical achievements which to earlier generations were evidence of man's greatness and a gage of his glorious future. They have exceeded anything dreamt of by their enthusiasts, but we, the presumed beneficiaries, watch them with intense *malaise*: conscious of man's powers having dangerously outdistanced his moral and spiritual development. As we gaze at the contrivers of Europe's desolation and debasement, an uneasy feeling insinuates itself, rising at times into an anguished conviction, that Hitler, Goebbels, and Streicher, the Third Reich with its doctrines, power, and conquests, its torture-chambers, death-trains, and vivisection practised on human beings, may not have been a gruesome accident or a monstrous aberration, but the correct consummation of the German era in history. Some 150 years ago Hölderlin described the Germans as 'barbarians of yore, rendered still more barbarous by their industry, science, and even by their religion'; and a young German who had watched German conduct in the first World War wrote to F. W. Foerster, one of the very few who dared protest, about his horror 'of men who are not human.'

What disturbing, nay alarming, connotations even seemingly innocuous terms of German self-appraisement have acquired for us! *Tüchtig, fleissig, sachlich, gehorsam* —they are all that, these efficient, hard-working, unimaginative, obedient robots who, because they have human shape, make one doubt man's fitness to wield anything more effective than a stone axe. Personalities of towering mind and character there have been among the Germans; yet the average, as individuals, are singularly devoid of individuality. A spiritual physiognomy they acquire only in groups, and change it with disconcerting suddenness according to the group which they enter, or into which they are fitted. They are imitative and responsive, and other men's suggestions, ideas, or inventions, taken over by them, have been developed, systematized, and applied with a thoroughness and resource which have put the German stamp on our age. Towards no people has the attitude of other nations varied so much in so short a time: a century ago, in England, France, and Russia alike, the Germans were regarded with an indulgence compounded of appreciation and contempt; twenty-five years later they astounded the world by their achievements, evoking admiration shot with anxiety; at the turn of the century they were the predominant power in Europe, conspicuous rather than respected; twenty-five years ago, defeated and discredited, they still managed to propitiate some of their near-victims and gain acceptance as objects for sympathy; and then for twelve years they oppressed mankind, terrorizing for the pleasure of striking fear and destroying with the savage joy of annihilation: a ghoulish nightmare. Crude, contorted, insane, but equipped with all the powers of modern technique, these 'unmerciful inventors of evil things' descended to levels never yet touched by man. And now the dream-play of the German century is over; the apocalyptic beast has vanished, it has disintegrated into shoals of astonishingly docile, obtuse, yet seemingly inoffensive individuals. Still, the Germans remain a sinister problem, an enigma of evil. If man's corruptible image can sink so low, what is our future, possessed as we are of powers never before at the command of man? Is anyone altogether free of that which in them has given authority unto the beast? And have not these germ-carriers assiduously propagated infection? Indeed, the bases of our past and the road we have traversed require re-examination. But the first object of the grand inquest must be the German nation.

War advances the sciences which devise its weapons; the quest for a better control of man thus armed must turn to the new 'humanities': foremost to history illumined by psychology and the social sciences, and directed to a pragmatic purpose. For while the historian at work should have no object other than the search for truth, this itself stands to gain by being carried on under the impelling and focusing urge of a practical need. It is therefore no disparagement to any history book to be called a *pièce d'occasion*, as which Mr. A. J. P. Taylor describes his own; in tracing 'The Course of German History,'[1] and surveying the development of Germany since 1815, he tries 'to answer the historian's question—how did this state of things come about?' Years of study, usefully recapitulated and tested in lectures and tutorials, have equipped him for the task; his book is written on material long garnered, and should prove of high value in the study of the German problem.

Rigid quiescence has for centuries been the prevalent style of German political life—there was little organic growth, and no generative revolution. In politics the German has proved uncreative and inept: change had to come mostly from outside. About 1520, Germany experienced the nearest approach to a spiritual and political upheaval: the Protestant Reformation bore the appear-

[1] *The Course of German History.* A Survey of the Development of Germany since 1815. By A. J. P. Taylor. Hamish Hamilton, 1945.

ance of a national movement fit to unite Germany. But
frightened by the Peasants' Revolt, Luther faltered, lost
faith in the people, took refuge under the wing of the
princes, and 'became the wild, unrestrained advocate of
a policy of absolutism and of ruthless repression.'
'Lutheranism, at first a movement of Reform, became,
and remained, the most conservative of religions; though
it preached the absolute supremacy of the individual
conscience within, it preached equally an absolute
supremacy for the territorial power without.' The great
spiritual travail of Reformation and Counter-Reformation left Germany divided against herself, the clash
between the claims of the individual conscience and of
the Universal Church being resolved by the ludicrous
formula of *cujus regio, ejus religio*: in favour of innumer-
able petty rulers, 'less restrained in internal affairs than
the greatest princes of Europe.' They were supreme, and
for almost 150 years after the Treaty of Westphalia the
unchecked absolutism of 'dynasties without roots or
substance' continued undisturbed from within, and protected by the balance of external forces—even the power
of the Habsburg Emperors was largely alien, being based
on Spain, Italy, and the Netherlands, on Bohemia and
Hungary, rather than on their German possessions. In
1789 there were 'two distinct Germanies—the Germany
of the two real powers, Austria and Prussia, and the
Germany of the unreal princes'; but the two powers
were on the periphery, and their capitals were border-
towns, while Central and Western Germany remained
politically inert, a beneficial shock-absorber ministering
to the tranquillity of the Continent. Of German national
consciousness a mere glimmer was kept alive in the
ecclesiastical States and the Free Cities, sham formations remote from real life. Extraneous intervention

was required to break through the coma of German politics.

'The French Revolution altered Germany only less profoundly than it altered France.' But while in that Revolution, which was 'greater than its greatest achievements,' the French people were craftsmen of their own fate, the Germans received its 'benefits—freedom of enterprise, equality before the law, security of property and of the individual, cheap efficient administration . . . without any exertion of their own.' 'Napoleon is often accused of having enslaved the Germans. His real fault lay in emancipating them. He did for the German liberals what they were never afterwards able to do for themselves.' Further, to subordinate Germany more effectively, he 'rationalized' her territorial structure, and by suppressing the ecclesiastical States, the Knights of the Empire, most of the Free Cities, and numerous other principalities, he reduced their number from more than two hundred to something above thirty, and thus heaved Germany a long distance towards unification, doing once more for the Germans what they were not fit to achieve themselves. Still, French intervention gave rise to 'a German nationalism, the sole quality of which was hostility to French rule'; this nationalism turned to Prussia, the only power reared in modern Germany: the Prussian myth was born in 1813.

Most nations have their borderers or backwoodsmen, rougher and more hardy than the long-settled populations of the sheltered homelands; Prussia is only one case among many. But while frontiersmen are as a rule an anarchic element, hardly ever fit to establish their ascendancy over the hinterland, the German settlers east of the Elbe built up a highly disciplined organization and State. By treating Prussia as extraneous and almost alien

to the rest of Germany, Mr. Taylor misses a vital point:
Prussia is essentially German, an emanation of Germany, her projection into the open spaces of North-
eastern Europe. That these were Slav or Lithuanian lands
conquered by the Teutonic Knights and colonized by
German peasants is hardly a sufficient explanation of the
enduring character of Prussia; by the time the Prussian
State was evolving its distinctive features, the aboriginal
populations of East Prussia and Brandenburg were as
little of a problem as the Cornish-speaking population in
the West of England. The aggressive spirit of Prussia
was rooted in the men rather than in circumstances.
Mr. Taylor remarks that when Frederick II forced
Prussia into the ranks of the Great Powers, 'this was no
"growth of Prussia," for it sprang from nothing . . .
except the King's will; it was a planned "making of
Prussia," as artificial as the making of a canal.' But the
same can be said about the work of at least two of
Frederick's predecessors. A will, a conception, an
organization, a State not bound up with any particular
territory but living in its army and for its army, this was
Prussia; truly German in its inception and development
(*Die Welt als Wille und Vorstellung*), and hence capable
of subjugating Germany politically and spiritually. In
the barren Baltic plain, the German spirit, stripped of
living symbols and organized tradition, and rendered
more austere by Lutheranism, unloaded itself in a
relentless drive for power; and these were the only
circumstances in which a German political synthesis was
feasible.

Mr. Taylor rightly scouts the legend of the Wars of
Liberation as a people's fight for freedom and self-
government. The number of volunteers was insignificant,
and the performance ran true to Prussian type. Stein

planned to raise German nationalist feeling against the French 'in a *jacquerie* organized from above,' while Scharnhorst and Gneisenau were not out to liberalize the Prussian State but to militarize the Prussian people; the system of education whereby this was done became 'the wonder of nineteenth-century Europe,' but was in reality 'a gigantic engine of conquest.' 'Service in the Prussian Army was the German version of service in the cause of liberty, and the defeat of the French at the Battle of Leipzig the German substitute for the fall of the Bastille.' Here Mr. Taylor touches upon a theme of paramount importance in German history. In 1808, Colonel Yorck declared that the Prussian peasant would undertake nothing without order from his King and without the big battalions; and more than 125 years later the Socialist leader Breitscheid, when asked in exile by an Englishman why the German working men had not resisted Hitler's assumption of dictatorial powers, took the blame: he had failed to give the order at the right moment! Apparently mass-action is only possible for the Germans in disciplined formations, under orders from above—unfree, and unfitted for freedom, they seek release in organized violence: war is the German version of revolution, an uplifting, liberating dispensation in which the nation finds its soul, while man surrenders his individuality in heroic self-immolation. One of Foerster's students wrote to him during the first world war: 'The important matter is to be ready to sacrifice oneself, not the *object* for which the sacrifice is made.' Scheler, Sombart, and other leading German intellectuals glorified the war in ecstatic terms, and rightly claimed that Germans alone could thus 'experience it.' In 1919 Spengler, having derided the pseudo-revolutionary 'hot-air merchants of Frankfort and Weimar,' concluded: 'A true revolution proceeds from an entire nation—in one cry, one iron grip, one rage (*Zorn*), with one goal. And this, the German Socialist revolution, occurred in 1914. It proceeded in legitimate and military forms [*Sie vollzog sich in legitimen und militärischen Formen*].' The emotional reaction of the German to war is *sui generis*, and it would be essential to trace its psychological determinants.

Mr. Taylor calls 1848 the decisive year of German history:

> For the first time since 1521, the German people stepped on to the centre of the German stage only to miss their cues once more. German history reached its turning-point and failed to turn. This was the fateful essence of 1848.

In February–March 1848, the triangular balance of France, Austria, and Prussia, on which the German Confederation of 1815 depended, was overthrown by revolutions in Paris, Vienna, and Berlin.

> The citizens of Germany—quite literally the established inhabitants of the towns—suddenly found themselves free without effort of their own. The prison walls fell, the gaolers disappeared. The Germany of intellectual conception suddenly became the Germany of established fact. . . . There was no successful revolution in Germany. . . . There was merely a vacuum in which the liberals postured until the vacuum was filled.

Fifty-one learned men met at Heidelberg and decided to convoke a Pre-Parliament. 'This strange nominated body conducted itself on the best parliamentary principles' and in friendly collaboration with the Federal Diet, representing the princes, arranged for the election of a National Assembly, which 'began its career with a background of respectability and legality.' Academic in character and distrustful of the masses, this gathering of notables aimed at achieving power by persuasion and at creating a united Germany by consent. An Executive was set up which 'had all the qualities of a government except power,' and became meaningless as soon as the military strength of Austria and Prussia was restored. 'To consider the causes of the failure of the German revolution is . . . a barren speculation. . . . There was . . . nothing to fail.' And although 'national Germany owed its temporary success to the defeat of the two military monarchies in March . . . it welcomed the reassertion of Austrian and Prussian military power' when directed against Bohemia and Posnania; the 'good Germans' evinced both their political ineptitude and their readiness to sacrifice liberalism to the inflated ego of modern nationalism. The German stage was set for Bismarck: Germany was to be 'conquered, not united.'

'Bismarck was a representative German, except that he had political sense.' He never aimed at uniting all Germans in a single national State—his programme was *Klein-Deutschland*, not *Gross-Deutschland*; the exclusion of Catholic Austria secured the preponderance of Lutheran Prussia, and rendered it possible for Germany to preserve her friendship with Russia on a common anti-Polish basis; whereas the inclusion of Austria would have burdened Germany with the nationality problems of a hopelessly ragged border, and the risk of a conflict with Russia over German interests and outposts in South-eastern Europe. So long as these liabilities and doubtful assets were left to the subsidiary firm in Vienna, Germany's frontier on a stretch of over a thousand miles—from Tilsit to Basle—was free of danger and vexations. Bismarck's policy was North-German, not Pan-German.

None the less, there was an inherent danger in Bismarck's Germany in that it knew no purpose but power for power's sake.

> Napoleon's armies marched under the banner of an idea, the German army under none. . . . Germany stood for nothing, except German power. . . . The highest faculties of the mind, and these the Germans possessed, were put to the service of a mindless cause.

Even their moral instincts, their asceticism and sense of duty were perverted—Foerster defines Prussianism as 'a highly developed morality in the service of . . . immorality, . . . Christianity in the service of Anti-Christ.' But whereas Bismarck put clear and strict limits to his system, William II, 'formed in the shadow of Germany's expanding and seemingly limitless might,' repudiated its essential precautions, and in so doing fell in with the prevalent mood of the German nation. In dominion over others the Germans were seeking an outlet for their overweening self-consciousness: they displayed the arrogance of wealth and power, the blatancy and deeper uneasiness of the *parvenu*, they indulged in verbal violence and yet attempted 'world policy on the cheap' (Hermann Bahr describes the modern German as 'a commercial traveller mimicking the gestures of Wotan'). Germany aspired to 'all the characteristics of greatness shown by others,' writes Mr. Taylor. Hence the demand for (useless) colonies, and for a great navy—its programme, 'a triumph of demagogy,' being carried through 'against the will both of the Foreign Office and of the General Staff' (but the Junkers and professional soldiers as villains of the piece remain the *fable convenue* of British opinion). *Die Wilhelminische Aera* passed into a 'strange period of interregnum.' 'A runaway horse or, more truly, an overpowered engine out of control—such was Germany in the last years of apparent peace.' Runaway in economic development, in population, in armaments, in political ambitions. So rapid was her growth that

> a little time must have brought both France and Russia, as it had already brought Austria-Hungary, into political and economic dependence. But for this Germany needed patience, tact, and political direction. She had none. German pride and German power demanded immediate results.

Threats were applied; next put into practice; and the World War became inevitable.

When the German front collapsed, constitutional government was 'made on the orders of the High Command. . . . Constitutional monarchy . . . was achieved without the effort, almost without the knowledge, of the German people; it was a manœuvre on the battlefield, not an event in domestic history.' Rathenau's dictum might appositely be quoted: 'Our chains were not broken, they fell off.' 'At the elections for the National Assembly, held on 19th January 1919, only two million out of thirty million voters supported the Independent Socialists, sole party of liberty and anti-militarism'—who, besides, were regionalists opposed to Prussian centralism. In February 1919, their governments in Bavaria, Saxony, and Brunswick were destroyed by the 'constitutional' parties working with the 'Free Corps' (forerunners of the Nazis). When the National Assembly met at Weimar, it was

> a repetition, almost a parody, of the Frankfort Parliament of 1848. In 1848 the liberals had owed their position, not to their own achievements, but to the breakdown of the old order. . . . In 1919 too the Weimar liberals owed nothing to their own efforts: they were the creation of Allied victory and were themselves protected from radicalism by the Free Corps. . . .

The Weimar constitution, mechanically 'most perfect of all democratic constitutions, full of admirable devices,' was the work of the Democrats, a party 'almost without backing, but possessing to the full the "spirit of 1848."' Even in the first republican Reichstag, elected in 1920, the Republic depended on an anti-republican majority; but it continued 'an ostensibly democratic, ostensibly pacific' life, be it with Hindenburg for President.

> In 1930 the last French troops left the Rhineland. . . . The victory of the Allied armies had brought the republic to birth . . . the evacuation of the Rhineland killed it. From start to finish the German republic, and the entire structure of German democracy, owed its existence to the supremacy of Allied arms.

'There was nothing mysterious in Hitler's victory,' writes Mr. Taylor. The mystery was rather that the German version of Fascism should have come so late.

> If Germany intended to undo the system of Versailles, she must organize for war, and she could organize for war only on a totalitarian basis. Only by renouncing foreign ambitions could Germany become a democracy; and as even the Social Democrats refused to make this renunciation the victory of the National Socialists was inevitable.

The 'Third Reich' was founded on terror; yet it represented 'the deepest wishes of the German people. In fact it was the only system of German government ever created by German initiative' and which owed nothing to alien forces. Here Mr. Taylor again treats Prussia as extraneous to Germany: had he said that the 'Third Reich' was the only democratic German government created by 'German force and German impulse,' his statement would be correct. Foerster wrote in 1941, in his book on *Europe and the German Question*:

From the democratic standpoint, Hitler is the most legitimate ruler Germany has ever had, a Kaiser who owes his crown to the most genuine popular vote. He is the spokesman of all the ideas held by the leading groups in Germany ever since 1850 . . . the logical expression of a century's illusion . . . which in National Socialism has donned the garb of primitive savagery and become the programme of Germany's renewal. Were a plebiscite held to-day, ninety per cent of the voters would vote for Hitler.

Having concluded his survey, Mr. Taylor confesses failure. 'Now that this book is written,' he says in the Preface, 'I find German history not only as distasteful but as mysterious as before: the explanations I have given convince my reason, but not my feelings'; and he notes with surprise that it occurs to none of the English historians 'educated in Germany and absorbed into German ways of thought . . . that there is anything strange in German history.' His disappointment and disconcertment seem to spring from the same source; he has carried his brilliant analysis to the border of psychological and sociological inquiry, without directly tackling the problem of what it is that makes the German behave in such, for us bewildering and incomprehensible, ways. Why do individual Germans in non-German surroundings become useful, decent citizens, but in groups develop tendencies which make them a menace to their fellow-men? This is a basic problem of German history, and the answer is of pragmatic importance.

We call the German 'inhuman': for sometimes he behaves like a beast, and sometimes like a robot. He is educated but not civilized. He can master 'in the highest degree the mechanical and intellectual side of civilization, altogether untouched by its spirit'—Mr. Taylor shows this dichotomy in Luther, Frederick II, Bismarck, in the Germans at large. Some 140 years ago, Mme de Staël, though she admired the Germans, commented on the incongruity between the elevation of their thoughts and the vulgarity of their habits: 'La civilisation et la nature semblent ne s'être pas encore bien amalgamées ensemble.' In 1827, Goethe remarked to Eckermann: 'We Germans are but of yesterday. . . . Several centuries may yet have to pass before our countrymen . . . can have it said of them: it is a long time since they were barbarians.' And on another occasion, thinking of the intellectual life of Paris, he ascribed German backwardness to geographical dispersion: 'We live such a miserable isolated life! . . . One of us sits in Vienna, another in Berlin, a third in Königsberg, a fourth in Bonn or Düsseldorf, hundreds of miles apart.' The perception of isolation was correct, but Goethe projected into space things which are of the spirit; if congregated the Germans are merely regimented: for the typical German is an introvert.

The Greek was a 'political animal,' the German is not. His political creations are inorganic and grotesque: in Brobdingnag as much as in Lilliput. They are the work of men with poor human contacts, isolated and tense: who require rigid rules and regulations in their intercourse with fellow-men, and, if forced into gregarious life, fit themselves into it to the point of self-annihilation, but cannot attain the culture of the *agora*. Stiff and stilted without ease or grace, the German has his 'code of honour' (and of duelling), his moral code, his primer of correct behaviour, even his notorious text-books of 'frightfulness.' Incapable of spontaneous adjustment, he must think and plan ahead: he does so with cold tenacity and works with bitter intensity. Introversion and divorce from reality produce a colossal, doctrinaire totalitarianism even in the realm of ideas: still, so long as the Germans remained *das Volk der Denker*, such peculiarities, at their worst, merely made them comic. But when these introverts were swept into action, when their inner tensions were translated into a supreme power-drive; when drunk with might they mistook their victories for a triumph of German *Kultur*, and (as Nietzsche foretold in 1873) the German mind was uprooted 'for the benefit of the German Empire'; when every accession of power rendered these latecomers more frantically envious of those who possessed the 'unbought grace of life,' while every frustration filled them with venomous rage: the world catastrophe was at hand. And when defeated and demented they developed a mass-movement, it assumed inhuman forms: from introverse isolation they plunged into the heat and intoxication of undifferentiated, uncritical mass-hysteria.

For in spite of their much-vaunted virility (the extreme concern for it suggests inner doubts), the Germans are strained, keyed up, overwrought: even Bismarck, their 'Iron Chancellor,' showed, as Mr. Taylor points out, symptoms of hysteria, with his 'screams and tears and breaking of jugs.' Their uneasy masculinity (which would never allow a German soldier in uniform to push a pram) leads to hero-worship and adoration of brute force: gentleness does not enter into the German concept of nobility. Nietzsche, who preached the 'superman' to the Germans, supplied in the description of his 'aristocrats' an accurate forecast of the Nazi war-criminals (*The Genealogy of Morals*, part I, para. 11):

. . . these same men, so severely kept in bounds by moral law, respect, custom, gratitude, and still more by mutual control. . . in relation to others, to the stranger or to a foreign country, do not differ much from beasts of prey let loose. They enjoy their release from social constraint, and seek outside its bounds compensation for the tension produced by long inclusion and adjustment in a peaceful community; they *revert* to the innocent beast-of-prey conscience, and turn into jubilant monsters who perhaps leave a ghastly scene of murder, arson, rape, and torture, in high spirits and with moral equanimity . . . convinced of having supplied the poets for times to come with a new theme for song and praise. . . . This is unmistakably the magnificent blond beast prowling after spoil and victory.

Some well-known Germans, as 'good Europeans,' have protested against such Nazi nihilism, and Rauschning, in *Hitler Speaks*, says of the sadistic pervert Roehm that he was 'an adventurer whose right place was in the colonies'!

2.

THE GERMAN MIND AND OUTLOOK

THE BOOK[1] consists of six papers given at the Institute of Sociology in 1942–3; and its object, according to Dr. Gooch, 'is to aid in the understanding of the gifted, efficient, hard-working, disciplined, romantic, unstable, inflammable and formidable nation with which for the second time in a generation we find ourselves at war.' While other contributors might have made a less appreciative choice of adjectives, or been more explicit about the origin of the two World Wars, none starts with an anti-German bias. Yet the upshot of their symposium verges upon an indictment, powerful because undesigned. The contributions emerge which the greatest German thinkers have, unwittingly, made to Nazism, and the nation is seen selecting, assimilating, and fusing them with a well-nigh unerring instinct: the mind and outlook behind this work of generations are fit to cause wonder if not despair. 'Pour chasser les démons, il faudrait un prophète,' said Louis-Philippe to Guizot. But prophets do not travel in the luggage-van of the conquering Allies.

Dr. Gooch supplies a systematic digest of 'German Views of the State,' and Professor Ginsberg an excellent survey of 'German Views of the German Mind.' Professor Willoughby's paper on 'Goethe and the Modern

---

[1] *The German Mind and Outlook.* By G. P. Gooch, Morris Ginsberg, L. A. Willoughby, E. M. Butler, S. D. Stirk, and Roy Pascal. With a Summary by Alexander Farquharson. Chapman and Hall. 1945.

World' exhibits the German at his best, but is hardly
relevant to a study of group mentality. Professor Eliza
Butler's brilliant essay on 'Romantic *Germanentum*' is a
work both of scholarship and art. Dr. Stirk, in 'Myths,
Types and Propaganda,' analyses the German *pseudologia
phantastica* from a new and interesting angle. Professor
Pascal's essay on 'Nationalism and the German Intellectuals' is not redundant, though it cannot avoid ground
covered in preceding essays.

'The form of democracy suitable for Germany has not
yet been found . . .' said Pastor Niemöller at a Church
Conference in September 1945. 'The German people
always leaned more towards being governed than govern-
ing themselves.' Indeed, self-government hardly enters
into the German concept of liberty. 'Few Germans,'
writes Dr. Gooch, 'asked for anything more than decent
government till the challenge of the French Revolution
compelled them to think.' And what then? Goethe maintained that 'the people had a right to be well governed,
not to govern themselves.' (He said to Eckermann on
18th January 1827: 'If a man has sufficient freedom to live
a healthy life and pursue his trade, that's enough, and so
much anyone can easily have.') Kant's political ideal was
not self-government but the *Rechtsstaat*, a State based
on the rule of law—'and by law he meant the fusing of
reason and morality.' Of practical reformers, Stein would
have corporations advise the King, while Hardenberg
said to Frederick William III: 'Your Majesty, we must do
from above what the French have done from below.'
Fichte responded at first to the ideas of the French Revolution, but soon lost himself in a nationalism described
by Professor Butler as the 'beginning of German megalo-
mania.' Hegel 'mistook the kingdom of Prussia for the
kingdom of heaven,' and, seeing in government 'a very

difficult task which requires highly skilled operators for
its success,' emphatically repudiated the sovereignty of
numbers.

The year 1848 was the *annus mirabilis* of German
liberalism. Dr. Gooch speaks of its 'generous inspiration,' quotes Heinrich von Gagern's 'ringing words'
about 'the sovereignty of the nation,' extols Arndt as one
of the veterans 'passionately devoted not only to Germany but to liberty,' and describes the failure of the
'Frankfort experiment' as a tragedy, 'for the tender
plant of German liberalism never recovered from the
shock.' But success might have been a worse tragedy, for
it would have shown up that unbridled nationalism under
whose impact the German counterfeit of Western liberalism broke every time the two conflicted in the Frankfort
Assembly. Might in a united Germany was the primary
concern of 'the men of 1848,' preachers of armed force
and war; national sovereignty was the obvious means
for overcoming the paralysing dynastic divisions; while
'liberty' was an adventitious consideration, and then it
was liberty for Germans only. Arndt passionately exhorted the Frankfort Parliament: 'Germans, be not too
just!' 'Treitschke,' writes Dr. Gooch, 'spans the transition from the aspirations of 1848 to the era of blood and
iron.' There was not much distance to span, and power
was readily accepted in lieu of self-government.

In the ideal State as conceived by Bismarck, the func-
tion of the representative assembly was to let off steam,
while the central place was assigned to 'a prudent
Chancellor with security of tenure.' Even Hans Delbrück,
one of the wisest German political writers of the pre-
1914 period, saw in democratic government merely a
fraud: a fraction of the community votes, the ruling
majority represents a still smaller part of the people, and

the system is worked by means of unscrupulous election campaigns. Tröltsch, scholar and thinker, in November 1918 spoke of German militarism as a political institution, 'the essence of a ruling society' in a system 'rendered tolerable by general well-being and a model bureaucracy'; had he remembered his Goethe and Hegel, he might have realized that this was all the Germans desired, but in the hour of defeat he thought that militarism 'had no roots in the people.' Still less had the Weimar Constitution.

Dr. Gooch, after stating that 'German democracy, which was born in the trenches, found expression in the Weimar Constitution,' concedes that, 'though the forms of democracy were there, they lacked the breath of life.' 'In the heart of the people,' wrote Spengler in 1919, 'the Weimar Constitution is already doomed. Its completion was received with utter indifference. . . . This episode is assured of the profound contempt of posterity.' He preached Caesarism as 'the instinctive revolt of the blood . . . of race-instinct, of the primitive will-to-power' —'in Spengler,' writes Professor Pascal, 'we see all the achievements of the great German culture . . . of its philosophy, its range of knowledge and depth of insight, put to the service of blind instinct, of brutal domination.' And close on him follow the conscious exponents of the Third Reich: 'If once the people feel that they have found a real leader,' wrote Moeller van den Bruck in 1923, 'they will joyfully accept his leadership and send to the devil all the democratic and socialist party chiefs whose impotence and selfishness they have long suspected.' The upshot of 150 years of German political thought was to be: 'Our Constitution is the will of the Führer.'

The territorial and social fragmentation of Germany,

as Professor Ginsberg points out, 'hindered the growth of a collective will'; Lutheranism, with its stress on faith and the inner life, and on obedience to constituted authority, contributed to Germany's *Entpolitisierung* (to her being rendered apolitical); and the Marxist doctrine that the advent of socialism is predetermined by the inner development of the capitalist system further reinforced the separation of thought and deed in German public life. Political formations, religions, and ideologies reflect the national character, and in turn stamp it with their pattern: in the tangled skein produced by the interplay of group mentality and historical circumstances it is well-nigh impossible to distinguish separate strands. But whatever the action of events on individuals or nations, the reaction is theirs: and facile extenuation is neither history nor psychology. Dr. Gooch pleads that Germany, 'a country with open frontiers, surrounded by unfriendly neighbours,' to become 'a nation-state like the rest' required 'a powerful Executive, a formidable army, and a disciplined people.' Yet the origin of Prussia is not in 'the Watch on the Rhine,' but in ruthless conquest of weaker neighbours across open frontiers; Italy, with the sea and high mountains for frontier, constantly suffered foreign invasion and rule, but produced Fascism when secure against both; while France, far more often overrun or threatened by enemies than Germany, never resorted to 'Prussianism.' 'Character is fate' is true of nations as much as of individuals.

What do the Germans think of their own mentality? On the intellectual side Professor Ginsberg finds them stressing the tendency to think in abstractions, which enables the German to soar high and search deep; but especially in social and political thought 'this lack of concreteness and an indulgence in fanciful abstractions' tend to produce 'a strange combination of vagueness and obscurity with profundity and comprehensiveness and a predilection for grandiose systems.' Hegel speaks of the German 'sense of natural totality': German totalitarianism started in the intellectual sphere. 'In the realm of feeling German writers lay stress on what they call depth, inwardness, inner warmth, indefinite but intense yearning or longing' (the German vocabulary abounds with terms of inner analysis and introspection). A tendency 'to depressive, uneasy, morose moods' is admitted, even to defeatism, 'occasionally submerged in a blare of bombast and self-stimulation.' Schopenhauer speaks of German *Schwerfälligkeit*, and Leibnitz of their *Gründlichkeit* —ponderosity and thoroughness are interconnected. Great stress is laid by German writers on the German's 'subjectivism': 'the power of the individual to make himself independent of the outer world' and to concentrate on his inner life. In short, the picture emerges of the perfect introvert; but Professor Ginsberg refrains from attaching the label.

Egocentrism produces a lack of measure and proportion (*Masslosigkeit*), and of inner poise and security. The German, 'dissatisfied with himself' and 'for ever worrying about his nature,' takes refuge in submission to authority and regulations, and comforts himself with the thought that freedom consists in the deliberate acceptance of self-imposed constraint. 'The lack of inner stability is . . . also reflected in the love of rank and outward distinctions'—Bismarck calls the Germans 'a race of non-commissioned officers,' eager for stripes, and possessed in public life of as much self-reliance as corresponds to each man's 'official hall-mark.' The ideological counterpart to this mentality is the deified Juggernaut State of Hegel and Treitschke, not subject to

any moral code but a law to itself; whose freedom of
action cannot be limited by rules; and to which the individual is sacrificed, or rather sacrifices himself. 'German
thinkers have at all times rejected all forms of utili-
tarianism and eudaimonism,' writes Sombart. 'The German "heroic" concept . . . looks on the State not as a
contrivance for happiness but as . . . a spiritual whole.'
And even Tröltsch sees society 'lifted above the world of
utility and material welfare.'

The psychological mechanism whereby the German
seeks in the prepotency of his State, and in dominion
over others, compensation for what he renounces as individual is indicated but insufficiently developed in the
book: power is to the German an extension of his impoverished yet inflated ego. Hence the 'mood of romantic
intoxication' which was generated by the victories of
Prussia, and the consequent *parvenu* mentality 'showing
itself in strident boastfulness and display, but at bottom
unsure of itself, fearful and resentful'; hence the *Real-
politik* and *Machtpolitik*, the brusqueness, arrogance, and
cold efficiency, 'mere masks hiding the old *Masslosigkeit*
and metaphysic.' Tröltsch speaks of a peculiar dualism
which after 1870 arose in German political thought:
'remnants of romanticism and lofty idealism' are blended
with 'a realism which goes to the verge of cynicism and
of utter indifference to all ideals and all morality'—the
result is a tendency 'to brutalize romance and romanti-
cize cynicism.' ('You must concede,' remarked Pastor
Niemöller at the Church Conference in September 1945,
'that Nazism in its early years had an almost spiritual or
mystic appeal—you cannot erase that from history.') The
morbid German romanticism 'which openly glorifies
violence and inculcates harshness and cruelty as ends
desirable in themselves' finds artistic expression in Stefan

George's remarkable poem 'The Burning of the Temple.'
In another poem George prophesied the coming of a
savage saviour and of 'a race of youths spewing far, far
away all that is soft and rotten, tepid and base'; but he
left Germany when the Third Reich was established.

Professor Ginsberg speaks about the truly remarkable
capacity of the Germans for self-intoxication and self-
deception, Professor Butler about their 'utter and in-
curable disregard of facts.' The fatal love for 'phantom
unreality' of idealist philosophers, though itself free of
sinister intentions, 'has led straight to that passion for
perverting truth which is so cynically preached and practised by the Nazis.' She traces back the origin of that
'ill-omened conception, romantic *Germanentum*,' to
Hölderlin, and still more to Fichte, who, with the help
of sweeping deductions and generalizations and of conclusions all-embracing and all-exclusive, purported to
prove that 'the Germans are inestimably superior to all
other European races'—he 'was not aiming at anything
so uninspiring as historical truth' but 'at realizing an
ideal which he had first invented, and then "discovered"
in the past.' Treitschke marks the next step in the
development of the myth: by the time he had 'impressed
his version of history . . . upon his fellow-countrymen a
grim and ghastly expression of hatred for other races was
becoming fixed on the visage of *Germanentum*.' But perhaps the most potent force for evil was Nietzsche, 'the
greatest writer with the sole exception of Goethe the
Germans have produced.' His superman was a compen-
sating myth, 'a smoke-screen' to the sickening reality
around (and within) him. But the ascent to a higher plane
he visualized through 'a species of highly aristocratic and
even austere jungle-law'; 'he aimed,' as Professor Pascal
puts it, 'at the heart of the democratic, humanistic way

of thinking'; he was out 'to destroy the very belief in the possibility of truth,' and 'led the onslaught on reason which has culminated in the Nazi ideology.' When preaching his *Herrenmoral*, he did not envisage the Germans as a *Herrenvolk*—whom '(deny it who will) he had relegated,' writes Professor Butler, 'to the lowest rung of the ladder of civilization—and wished to de-Germanize at all costs.' Yet his teaching greatly swelled the torrent of the *Germanentum*.

> Fichte had persuaded the Germans that they were the chosen people; Nietzsche preached a gospel of power; add those two things together; subtract Fichte's will to peace and Nietzsche's scorn of the German race, multiply by brutality and vulgarity and the sum of Nazi ideology comes out. And somehow Nietzsche's responsibility seems to loom large. . . .
>
> By the time Houston Stewart Chamberlain, Alfred Rosenberg, and Hermann Wirth had invented and discovered the 'Aryan' race, Nietzsche's mythological superman had found a local habitation and a name.

'The finishing touches to romantic *Germanentum*, that monster of unreality,' were put by Stefan George. Had Coleridge, after writing 'Kubla Khan,' exhorted 'his fellow-countrymen to discover the River Alph, and to heed the ancestral voices prophesying war,' it would have made little difference. But not so in Germany, where myths are deliberately cultivated.

The word 'myth,' Dr. Stirk points out, has a different meaning in English from what 'Mythos' has acquired in German. In Fowler it is 'little more than a tale devoid of truth or non-existent person or theory or event'; but in Brockhaus, 'a symbolic idea with life-renewing force'; and according to Gundolf, 'myth is the word and vision of *Volk* and God, of real happenings.' From doubts about reality the Germans have advanced to the belief 'that ideas do not and need not have any relationship to truth and facts, but are fully justified if they promote the interests of those who hold them' (see Professor Pascal on Vaihinger). And in defeat the Germans turned more than ever to myths—a 'mythical madness seemed at times to come over them,' writes Dr. Stirk. Wagner, Nietzsche, and George were their spiritual leaders, all three in opposition to bourgeois life and outlook, in 'revolt against reason,' and in search for a myth; and 'National Socialism . . . seems to have achieved a union of the worst elements in each, and to have thrown the good in each of them overboard.' 'Millions suddenly realize,' writes Alfred Rosenberg, 'that it is their task to experience a myth and to create a type. And out of this type to build the State and to shape their lives.'

As with 'myth' so with 'type': in English it is hardly a compliment to call someone 'a type,' but post-war Germany added to hero-worship a worship of types (collective self-adoration): both 'a wonderful preparation for Hitler and National Socialism.' There was *der heldische Mensch* (the heroic man), the Prussian type, *der Frontsoldat* (the front-line soldier), the Worker—'all essentially masculine and virile; . . . all "fighters" and warriors; . . . all anti-bourgeois; they all arose out of the First World War, and found their natural fulfilment in the Second.' Sombart, one of the foremost German economic and *Kultur*-historians, wrote in 1915: 'To be German means to be a hero'; Germans regard war 'as the most holy thing on earth'; 'the chosen people of this century is the German people.' And here is a discourse by Ernst Bergmann, Professor of Philosophy at Leipzig (1934):

What is heroic? Heroic is God. . . . Heroic was the Yule God, the divine Man of Light of the prehistoric North.

Heroic is Odin, the Germanic God of Knowledge. And heroic is the man of Kant and Fichte. Heroic is the man who sacrifices himself for his *Volk* in war and peace. . . . And heroic is the mother who bears children for her *Volk*. Heroic is the Führer who believes in his *Volk* and its heroic greatness! Heroism is the natural form of the German-Nordic man.

Or Rosenberg's glorification of the *Frontsoldat*:

The faces under the steel helmets in the War Memorials have all a well-nigh mystical similarity. A high, furrowed brow, a strong, clear-cut nose, tightly closed lips. . . . The eyes, wide-open, look straight ahead. Conscious of the distance, of eternity. This strong-willed manliness of the front-line soldier differs widely from the ideal of beauty of earlier times. . . . But this new beauty is also peculiar to the German worker, indeed to the striving German of to-day.

'War was of the very essence . . . of the myths and types,' concludes Dr. Stirk. What Hitler and the Nazis did was to drum these ideas into the German people 'with the help . . . of a masterly, relentless propaganda.'

Many a reader will close the book feeling that there is such a thing as a Belsen of the mind and the spirit.

3.

EAST-CENTRAL EUROPE

IN 1918 the older dreams of 'liberty, equality, and *bisque d'homard'* reappeared in East-Central Europe as a programme of 'national self-determination, democracy, and agrarian reform.' These principles, solemnly proclaimed and partially realized, reshaped the territorial, political, and social configuration of the region that intervenes between Germany and Italy in the west, and Russia in the east—the zone of small nations. A stocktaking of results is now attempted by Mr. Hugh Seton-Watson in his book *Eastern Europe Between the Wars, 1918–1941*[1]; leaving aside the northern and southern fringes—the four Baltic States, Albania, and Greece—he concentrates on the six States which form the core of that zone: Czechoslovakia, Poland, Hungary, Rumania, Yugoslavia, and Bulgaria. The description of 'East-Central Europe' would seem more appropriate for them when viewed apart from Russia: for whatever her relations to the rest, it is her vast shape which fills the picture evoked by the geographical term of 'Eastern Europe.'

In 1938 the joint population of these six States was about 100 millions, of whom almost 30 millions were unwilling, or unwanted, 'national minorities'; they formed roughly one-third of the population in Poland, Czechoslovakia, and Rumania, one-fifth in Yugoslavia and Hungary, and almost one-seventh in Bulgaria. Moreover, in

[1] *Eastern Europe Between the Wars, 1918–1941.* By Hugh Seton-Watson. Cambridge University Press. 1945.

Czechoslovakia and Yugoslavia the 'State-nationality' was composite, consisting of Czechs and Slovaks, of Serbs, Croats, Slovenes, and Bosnian Muslims (really a fourth branch of the Yugoslav nation). Three of the States were overwhelmingly, and two predominantly, agricultural, the peasants forming in Bulgaria 80 per cent of the population, in Yugoslavia 75, in Rumania 78, in Poland 63, in Hungary 55, and in Czechoslovakia 34 per cent. Vitiated 'self-determination' put a strain on 'democracy' among the beneficiaries as well as among the aggrieved; and 'agrarian reform' itself became an instrument of warring nationalisms.

Czechoslovakia, though in many ways an integral part of East-Central Europe, differs widely from the other five States. The Czechs had by 1918 attained a Central or West European level in education, professional training, and political maturity. They had a balanced social structure, 'a prosperous and experienced bourgeoisie . . . a trained and disciplined working class and a reasonably well educated and organized peasantry.' 'The Austrian tradition of honest and fairly efficient administration was continued,' and Czechoslovakia 'was the only State east of Switzerland and south of the Baltic which for twenty years preserved political liberties and progressive social institutions.' This favourable record ('only the Czechs have something good to look back to')

is in great part due to the Liberal and humanitarian tradition of the Czech people . . . personified in the modern Czechoslovak Republic by the President-Liberator, Thomas Masaryk. This truly great man . . . more than once . . . made himself unpopular by standing up against militant ignorance, prejudice and chauvinism, but in the end his people realized that he was right, and repaid him with a veneration and love which few statesmen have received. . . .

Czechoslovakia, though not untainted by doctrines of nationalism, applied in the cultural and economic fields, was 'the country . . . which most consistently defended a foreign policy based on Democracy, which most sincerely worked for solidarity of East European nations, which treated its minorities most humanely. . . .' 'Its fall was not only a strategical but a moral loss to Europe.'

Even the Germans, 'unreliable citizens' who 'regarded themselves as the race appointed by God to rule in Bohemia,' who 'despised the Czechs, and could never admit them to a status of equality with themselves, still less accept subordination to them,' suffered very little that could be called persecution. There was petty chicanery by local officials, and a measure of economic discrimination. German industries suffered through the changes of frontier in 1919 and the economic depression of the 'thirties, but the Prague Government was

less interested in restoring the fortunes of German enterprises, many of which were directed by men known as implacable enemies of the Republic, than in creating a highly skilled Czech industry. Government contracts were given to Czech firms rather than to German, Czech workers were employed in preference to German, and not much was done for the relief of the German unemployed.

On the other hand, an honest attempt at political cooperation was made at the centre: from 1926 onwards the chief German political parties were regularly conceded seats in the Czechoslovak Government—which did not prevent the rise of a most venomous Nazi movement. In the general election of 1935, Henlein's 'Sudetendeutsche Partei' obtained two-thirds of the German vote in Czechoslovakia. In view of what happened in the

Czech provinces after Munich and Prague, and during the war, 'it is hardly credible that the two nations can be friends again.'

While the Czech provinces were West European in structure and outlook, Slovakia was part of the wider Balkans, and Carpatho-Russia probably the most backward district in East-Central Europe. In these two countries the Czechs had to contend with the evils of rural overpopulation, of an inferior peasant agriculture, and of a poorly balanced social structure; and with an even worse lack of mental balance in the educated and semi-educated classes. Undoubtedly the Czechs committed mistakes; promises of autonomy were not properly kept, and the behaviour of the Czech officials was not always tactful. But Czech administration was highly beneficial and achieved a marked improvement in the economic and cultural sphere. When Serbia and Rumania took over former Austrian and Hungarian provices, 'a primitive "Oriental" State acquired large areas accustomed to more advanced standards of administration'; in Poland, a western, a semi-western, and an eastern area 'struggled against each other . . . without decisive results, although . . . on balance . . . Oriental standards prevailed'; in Czechoslovakia alone eastern provinces came under a western administration. Still, material gains do not necessarily secure popularity or assuage chauvinisms, and the experiences of the Czechs in both provinces were far from pleasant or encouraging.

'The Land Reforms were not economic measures, and cannot be judged as such.' They were instruments of national policy or were enacted under pressure from the peasant masses, and were most radical where the upper classes were foreign or estranged from the nation. The

big landed estates of the Magyars in the provinces
detached from Hungary, or of the Germans in Upper
Silesia, Bohemia, and Moravia, had been the mainstay of
an alien social superiority and political dominion, and
their transfer to the native peasantry was of vital interest
to the new States. On the contrary, it would have been
against the interest of the Polish State to carry through
an honest agrarian reform in the so-called 'Eastern Borderlands,' for this would have destroyed the influence of
the Polish manor houses and handed over the land to
White Russian or Ukrainian peasants. In Hungary proper
and in ethnic Poland, where landowners and peasants
were of the same nationality, extensive measures of
agrarian reform were planned at first, but they shrank
or were shelved after the danger of social revolution had
receded and authoritarian Governments had become
firmly established.

But even where carried out thoroughly, the Land
Reforms failed to justify the hopes that they 'would solve
the Peasant Problem, and that the masses, socially satisfied, would form a stable basis of the State. . . . By 1939
the situation of a large part of the Eastern European
peasantry was worse than it had been in 1914.' Who of
us has not heard stories about the sturdy individualism
of the peasant and about property in land which changes
sand into gold, 'romantic nonsense about the stern virtues of the soil-loving peasants, and sentimental rhapso-
dies about their beautiful costumes'? Anyone acquainted
with the economic structure and life of the East-European village could have foreseen or guessed what Mr.
Seton-Watson has discovered; but still it is a relief to find
a writer, neither a 'feudal reactionary' nor a 'Communist,' talking sense about peasant agriculture. Thus:
'Even the most casual visitor is impressed by the differ-

ence in quality of the crops he sees on a drive through a region such as the Wallachian plain, where small holdings and large estates exist side by side.' And further: in Eastern Europe, as a rule, 'the smaller the holding the lower the productivity of the soil.' But in 1939 almost three-fourths of the peasant holdings in the six States of East-Central Europe were under five hectares (roughly 12½ acres), and were, as a rule, inadequate for the maintenance of a peasant family; they comprised about one-fourth of the cultivable land. Even the medium-sized holding produced mainly for self-consumption: and the peasant's staple food is cereals, for which large farms are best suited. The parcelling out of the big holdings or the surviving estates would be a mere palliative if the system of peasant agriculture remained unchanged.

In Eastern Europe the peasants live mostly in clustered villages, and their land consists of scattered strips in the open fields (the opposite system is of scattered homesteads joined to consolidated farms). The separation of the homestead from its land encourages endless subdivision, which tends to break up self-sufficient farms into uneconomic dwarf holdings; moreover, the peasant often owns his land in strips miles apart from each other, and of prodigious length but only a few yards wide. Land and labour are wasted in unproductive agriculture.

'The fundamental problem of the Eastern European peasantry in all small-holder regions is over-population.' The pressure on the land in Poland, Rumania, Yugoslavia, and Bulgaria 'is more severe than in Italy, and very much more severe than in Germany,' and they have a 'far better right to call themselves "proletarian nations."' Denmark has 36·6 people per square kilometre of cultivable land, Hungary 80·6, Rumania 116·3, Bulgaria 119, Yugoslavia 157·4; but in Denmark the

yield of wheat per hectare is 29·2 quintals and in Yugoslavia 11, where consequently 'on a given unit of land
four times as many people produce three times less
wheat than in Denmark.' It is not merely that their work
is less productive: the great majority of all small-holders
in Eastern Europe are permanently underemployed.
Mr. Seton-Watson calculates that in Poland, Rumania,
Yugoslavia, and Bulgaria, one-third of the available man-
power is wasted, or to give a total numerical equivalent,
'more than 17,000,000 peasants are unemployed.' Emigration is the first obvious remedy; industrialization of
those countries is another; but most essential of all is a
thorough rationalization of peasant agriculture. Land has
been parcelled out to peasants who have neither the
technical knowledge nor the technical equipment to
maintain a satisfactory system of production; collective
or co-operative forms of agriculture must render possible once more an efficient cultivation of crops which
require wide spaces (but the Governments of East-
Central Europe shunned any such approach to the
problem, denouncing it as 'Bolshevik,' and congratulated themselves on the peasants being 'fortunately
immune to Communist ideas'). A reconsolidation of
holdings might moreover lead to a better selection of
crops and give scope for the employment of agricultural
experts—perhaps more sons of peasants would then
study agriculture and fewer go in for law and politics.

So much for the *bisque d'homard* of 1918—but what
of 'equality,' or its 1918 equivalent, peasant democracy?
King Carol and the Iron Guard, King Boris and the
I.M.R.O. or some military group, King Alexander and
Stoyadinović were not the heroes of those dreams, nor
were Beck and Smigly-Rydz, Gömbös and Imrédy. 'It

is pointed out,' writes Mr. Seton-Watson, 'that in Rumania, Yugoslavia, and Bulgaria the majority of the ruling class consists of sons of peasants. This is true but unimportant.' In the Balkans 'the fondest dream of every able young son of a peasant' is to become an official; but, having risen, he feels 'immeasurably superior' to the class from which he has sprung. Moreover,

the 'sons of peasants' who become Ministers or business men are almost always sons of big holders, schoolmasters, or priests, of the 'rural bourgeoisie'. Few are sons of one of the small·holder families which form 70 per cent of the agrarian population of Eastern Europe.

The gap between rich and poor peasants widened during the agricultural depression of the 'thirties, the 'kulaks' stepping into the place of the big landowners. The big peasant was no check on the *nouveaux riches* of those countries, the jobbing, grafting politicians: he was a thorough social reactionary. In 1918, 'the prospects of an organized peasantry as a political force seemed bright'; 'outwardly impressive movements were built up.' The expectations attached to them were to be disappointed. The Peasant Parties almost invariably represented the narrow interests of the wealthy peasants, and while prating 'about a special Peasant Democracy,' they ignored the interests, nay the very existence, of the vast masses of rural proletarians.

Some of these parties were rendered helpless by terror exercised from above (Bulgaria and Poland). Others collapsed from internal decay (Serbia and Rumania). Others came under the control of the urban bourgeoisie (Czechoslovakia) or of nationalist intellectuals (Croatia).

In Czechoslovakia, the freest and least corrupt of the six States of East-Central Europe,

the Agrarian Party was always in power . . . it took part
in coalition after coalition. . . . It was the dominant party.
. . . Its political success attracted to it various elements
that had little in common with the peasant class . . . it
was in a position to offer personal material advantages to
all its supporters . . . [it] became an 'Interessengemein-
schaft' of people eager for political and economic spoils.

During the last years of the Republic it was 'the main
party of capital,' in close touch with the biggest Czech
bank. When the national catastrophe supervened, its
political record required a euphemism to be described
as merely poor.

In Rumania the National Peasant Party, when in
power, favoured the bigger peasants and did next to
nothing for the mass of the poor; its most important
measure was to 'throw open the country to foreign
capital,' which won its leaders 'the undying affection of
British, French, and American capitalists.' The country
benefited, and some of the Ministers 'made fortunes with
striking speed.' 'In Eastern Europe,' writes Mr. Seton-
Watson in a different connection, 'the greatest fortunes
are made not in industry or banking but in politics'—
but this applied to other parties even more than to those
of the peasants. After 1934, 'a number of promising
young National Peasants were cajoled, or bought by
money or favours, into the king's camp,' and Maniu
(personally incorruptible) 'found himself gradually abandoned . . .' In 1937 he finished by making an inexcusable
electoral pact with the Iron Guard, which demoralized
his best supporters.

In Serbia the Radical Party, once turbulently democratic, after 1918 'became increasingly Conservative, and
soon definitely placed the interests of the bourgeoisie
before those of the peasantry.' The Croatian Peasant

Party, 'originally a social revolutionary movement,' gradually changed into 'a nationalist organization directed by the urban middle class'—an 'uneasy marriage of peasant democrats and bourgeois reactionaries.'

Still, the story of the Peasant Parties is but part and parcel of the moral and spiritual *dégringolade* of the *intelligentsia* in at least five out of the six countries of East-Central Europe, and of the poor part they played as politicians, bureaucrats, business or professional men—in short, as rulers of the new States. The malformation started with the universities. The students, mostly sons and daughters of poor families, should have formed the élite of these young nations, but did not. 'A number of excellent young men and women completed their training every year, but they seldom formed a very high percentage.' The Czech universities were the best, the Hungarian had 'a fairly good record,' the Serb students rendered service to the cause of political freedom. 'The lowest level . . . was that of the Polish and Rumanian universities. . . . In Poland bands of anti-Semitic and Fascist students were used by the National Democratic Party to embarrass the Government, and by the Government against Socialists, Democrats, and National Minorities.' In Rumania 'the University of Jassy, capital of Moldavia, supplied the police with a number of students willing to earn an honest penny as toughs, *agents-provocateurs*, strike-breakers or Jew-baiters'—the original Iron Guard. 'The false educational system of Eastern Europe, which at the best encouraged chauvinism and at the worst helped to destroy all conceptions of morality, is one of the fundamental causes of the misfortunes of these peoples.'

But is it possible to separate the 'educational system' from the general pattern of life in those countries? There were deep divisions and bitter hatreds, fostered by a 'pernicious spirit of romantic nationalism,' by 'training in chauvinism,' and a brutalization not confined to East-Central Europe. With it went the vainglory and cheap nationalist *hubris* of the half-educated. 'The ruling class of the Old Kingdoms of Serbia and Rumania . . . considered that they had "liberated" the new provinces,' and expected gratitude and deference, to which the Slovenes, Croats, Transylvanians, and Bukovinians replied by declaiming interminably about the superiority of their own culture, and by denouncing the Serbs and Rumanians as 'Byzantine barbarians' or 'Orientals.' 'The battle for economic and administrative control was fought fiercely between Bucharest and Transylvania.' 'The antagonism of the Croats . . . against all Serbs only increased with the passage of time.' In Poland, Yugoslavia, and Rumania alike, backward areas with alien populations 'became the victims of merciless exploitation and police brutality,' till even potentially loyal parts of the population were turned 'into real Communists and Separatists.' There was corruption in high places. 'Taxes were collected with ruthless brutality.' There was 'no redress against administrative abuses.' 'Oppression, robbery, discontent, and disunity were greater throughout Eastern Europe in 1939 than they had been in 1918.'

One by one the last traces of 'Democracy' disappeared, and pseudo-Parliamentarianism gave way to police dictatorships or Fascist régimes. . . . Freedom, prosperity, and power were confined to members of the ruling gang. Fine proclamations were issued about National Unity, Moral Regeneration, Non-Party Objectivity, and Strong Hands. . . . These 'strong Governments' were no more than greedy, corrupt, and brutal class régimes, which did not feed but fed upon their peoples. . . .

'Class régimes'? But how much 'class' had there ever been, or has survived, in most of these countries? Mr. Seton-Watson explains that although 'the ruling classes of Eastern Europe do not contain so many millionaires as those of the West—the contrasts of wealth are more striking, for the bottom level is lower, and on it sit more than half the people.' Is this a sufficient explanation? In Bulgaria there was a 'comparative absence of striking contrasts in wealth,' a much larger proportion of medium holdings and an utter absence of large estates—'a healthier property structure in agriculture'; moreover, 'defeat . . . deprived the ruling class of the opportunities for enrichment that existed in the victorious small States.' And yet 'Bulgaria has suffered from the same bitter division between rulers and ruled that afflicted her neighbours.'

The ruling class of civil servants, army officers, tradesmen and intellectuals jealously maintained by force their supremacy over the people. The peasants and workers . . . wished to wrest political power from their masters . . . and the bitterness of the passions aroused on both sides is proved by the ferocity with which the attempt was repressed. Torture was regularly used in all the Eastern European States, but none has a record of such systematic and uninterrupted brutality as Bulgaria.

Thus there was neither 'feudalism' nor 'capitalism,' merely the never-ending insolence of those in power. Mr. Seton-Watson, almost unconsciously, sums up the East European scene in an incidental remark: 'A peasant who did not like to have his daughters raped or his property stolen by a gendarme' was treated as 'a Bolshevik.' It suffices for a man to rise one rung off the ground, and to put on an official uniform, even that of a gendarme, to create the contrast of rulers and ruled; and the

position is not improved by the 'ruler' being brutish
and new to the pleasures of wielding authority.

Mr. Seton-Watson remarks on 'the strange fact' that
Hungary, which was the first to experience White Terror,
and 'where the people had fewer rights and liberties,'
retained 'remnants of Liberalism' (or rather of a constitutional régime), and he pays tribute to Count Teleki,
the Prime Minister who committed suicide when the
Regent and the General Staff forced Hungary into war
on the side of the Axis: 'however little one may approve
his reactionary outlook, however clearly one may see the
fatal defects of the régime he represented, it is impossible
to withhold sympathy from an honourable man.' Still,
'these rulers belong to the past. Pre-capitalist Conservatism is an attractive phenomenon, but it has no
place in the modern world.' This may be so: it probably
is so. But the East European Lavals and Déats, or coun-
terfeits of Hitler and Mussolini, 'democratic' products
of the capitalist and still more of the post-capitalist era,
are as unattractive as their Central or West European
confrères and models.

'Is Democracy possible in Eastern Europe?' asks
Mr. Seton-Watson; and he replies: 'What the people
want is more to eat, more land, more justice, more personal security,' whereas 'experience has shown that
despotisms do not generally give the people these things.'
But can such a conviction, however strong, give them the
capacity for a 'democratic' régime? The problem is not
limited to East-Central, or even Eastern Europe. All
government is based on some form of oligarchy: and the
moral and intellectual level of the men who compose it
and the view they take of government and their responsibility towards the governed matter far more than their
social origins. The first and most elementary requirement

in government is a routine of decent administration. When endowed with moral values of a religious, national, or class character, such a routine is called tradition. Self-made men (or imported kings) can continue a tradition, but cannot, on the strength of being 'self-made,' create one. Wars and revolutions have broken up routines, and 'intellect' has corroded traditions: Mr. Seton-Watson's book is a study in the life and habits of *ersatz* 'ruling classes.' The old ruling classes have practically disappeared on the European continent: they perished mostly because they were not equal to their task; but even so their countries are the poorer.

4.

YUGOSLAVIA

I

THE STRUCTURE of the non-national Habsburg Monarchy was upheld by the dreary maze of national problems inside, and across, its borders. Each problem was a perplexing tangle, and, with the exception of the Serbs, every nationality, even if opposed to the existing order and régime, had to count with the danger of greater evils were Austria-Hungary to collapse. It was the unique position of the Serbs with regard to the survival of the Dual Monarchy which explained the uncompromising hostility of Vienna and Budapest against them.

The Dual Monarchy secured the predominance of the Germans in Western Austria, the rule of the Poles in Galicia, and of the Magyars over historic Hungary. Hitler's forerunners, the Pan-Germans, were prepared to break up the Habsburg Monarchy in order to merge Western Austria into a Greater Germany: their aim was Pan-German union, and complete dominion over Czechs and Slovenes. Others, especially those whose German nationalism was diluted with Austrian patriotism, preferred the wider advantages of an Empire and an army which entwined some forty million non-Germans in an alliance with Germany, placed them (in varying degrees) under German influence, and safeguarded the German minorities among them. Magyar nationalists of the Kossuth school continued to clamour for Hungary's complete independence. Far-seeing Magyars, followers of Deák, Andrássy, and Tisza, while guarding jealously against any revival of an Imperial Austrian centralism, realized the signal advantages which the Dual Settlement, their own creation, secured for the Magyars, one of the smallest of nations: dominion over an at least equal number of non-Magyars in Hungary, control over the policy of a Great Power, and hence the position of a partner in the (for them indispensable) German alliance—not, as in 1938–45, of a very inferior dependant. The Roman Catholic Poles, oppressed by Protestant Prussia and Greek-Orthodox Russia, and hostile to both, enjoyed national freedom under the Habsburgs, and dominion over the Little Russians of East Galicia: they could not wish for a break-up of the Habsburg Monarchy if this were to place them under Russia. The simple problem of the Italian irredenta in the Trentino was complicated by the interests of the Italian minorities on the Adriatic coast, and the position of Italy as a member of the Triple Alliance.

Of the subject races, the Czechs and Slovaks had no territory outside the Habsburg Monarchy, and their nearest friend was Russia: but democratic or Catholic, they were not altogether congenial to Greek Orthodox Tsarism. Moreover, a break-up of the Habsburg Monarchy might have engulfed the Czechs in a Greater Germany, and the Slovaks in a fully independent Hungary. The Little Russians of East Galicia, the Bukovina, and Carpatho-Russia, were Uniats; the 'Uniat' Church and 'Ukrainian' nationalism, originally fostered by the Poles, had turned against them, but remained anti-Russian, and therefore pro-Austrian. Ruman irredentism in Transylvania and the Bukovina was complicated by Rumania's anti-Russian policy: she was

Greek-Orthodox but not Slav, and her Hohenzollern King, Charles I (1866–1914), was pro-German. There is no difference of language between Croats and Serbs, and little between them and the Slovenes, but the Croats and Slovenes are Roman Catholics. Divided by religion and traditions from the Serbs and Russia, the Croats retained pro-Habsburg leanings even after having been sacrificed by the dynasty to the Magyars. In a break-up of Austria the Slovenes had to fear inclusion in a Greater Germany and a Greater Italy.

On this balance of incompatibilities and fears rested Austria-Hungary's ramshackle existence; it was uninspiring yet tolerable so long as it remained negative and unaggressive: it was a condition and not a cause—few could feel devotion for it, but few were ready wilfully to upset it. Any positive exertion or strain was bound completely to transform or to destroy it.

The challenge to Austria-Hungary's existence, answered by an equally unsettling self-assertion, came from the Serbs. They alone in no way profited by the existence of the Habsburg Monarchy, and had nothing to fear from its collapse. Slav and Greek-Orthodox, therefore singlemindedly pro-Russian, they were hostile to the Magyars and unconnected with the Habsburgs. From Germany and Italy they were separated by Croat and Slovene territories. The Serbs of Dalmatia, Bosnia and Herzegovina, of Slavonia and Southern Hungary, wished for national reunion in a Greater Serbia. But in all these unredeemed territories they lived intermixed with Croats and Slovenes. The programme of a Great Serbia was soon expanded and merged into that of a Yugoslavia comprising Serbs, Croats, and Slovenes; this reproduced complications and contradictions such as beset Austria-Hungary and were fostered by her existence (which was like a drug, alleviating grave conditions, aggravating milder ones). In the course of centuries, the compact block of Yugoslav territory had been broken into fragments. In 1910, Yugoslavs inhabited several small Austrian provinces; Croatia, with an old Constitution and Diet, and the Free City of Fiume, both connected with Hungary; the Banat and Bacska incorporated in Hungary; Bosnia and Herzegovina under a joint Austro-Hungarian régime; the two independent Kingdoms of Serbia and Montenegro; and Old Serbia and Serb Macedonia still under the Turks. This was an untenable situation, yet threatening to burden any new settlement with the chequered past and its problems; and it was the endeavour of Austria-Hungary to perpetuate, widen, and envenom existing divisions—a further provocation to the Serbs. A showdown between the Habsburg Monarchy and the Yugoslavs, especially the Serbs, was unavoidable.

Austria-Hungary had come to serve as channel for imparting Western civilization to Serbia in a corrupt and corrupting version: its shoddiest produce was exported to the Balkans. Blended with the semi-Asiatic heritage of the Ottomans in decay, and suffused with a belated revolutionary romanticism, it produced distasteful results in Serbia's political life. But as in turn information about her reached Western Europe mainly through Austrian channels, episodes in the lives of the last Obrenovitches and their end, or the drama of Sarajevo, were skilfully exploited against her. Hardly another rising, or renascent, nation had so great an array of enemies and so few friends. Habsburgs, Austrians, Magyars, and Italians, were united in their hostility to the Serbs; and Roman Catholics, pro-Habsburg and pro-Croat, disliked the Serbs as champions of the Croats almost more than as their opponents. Russia might have been expected to befriend the Serbs: but the Bulgars, her vanguard against Constantinople, were her favourites: for a long time she failed to perceive that whatever the feelings of the people, the conflict with Serbia was converting Bulgaria into a tool of the Central Powers. In Great Britain, till some thirty years ago, there were pro-Turks and pro-Bulgars (as in 1876–8), but very few pro-Serbs.

Serbia's performance in the First World War secured for her a place of honour. But even greater was the heroism and self-sacrifice of the Serb nation in March 1941. The danger which threatened us in September 1938 is still quoted as justification for Munich—could anyone who pleads that excuse blame the Serbs had they failed to rise against their appeasers? They were surrounded by enemies; had a good many in their own midst; could expect little help from outside; were clearly unprepared for mechanized war; had no Channel to protect them against the German impact; and had seen the use to which the *Luftwaffe* was put in Warsaw and Rotterdam. A longer resistance may have been expected: but about the outcome and its aftermath in suffering, there could be no doubt. Still, the Serbs revolted for their country's honour, and went into battle: *more Serbico*.

2

What people were these, what was the nature of their country, what was their past, what were their treasures, their modes of living, their difficulties, and their inspiration? No political or historical treatise, no specialized inquiry, could have supplied even the beginning of an answer. A living picture is required of the land and the nation, a record of human impressions, emotions, perceptions, and thoughts, gathered into one; the kind of work for which there is no formula before it is attempted, and of which no summary can be given after it is accomplished. This is what Rebecca West has achieved in her book *Black Lamb and Grey Falcon*[1], described as 'The Record of a Journey through Yugoslavia in 1937.' There is no more system or completeness in it than in the colour-scheme of wild flowers in a field: but there is great beauty, and it lives. Little evidence appears of gardening or weeding;[2] it is not without faults; it is digressive and long; still, were I asked what I should like changed or omitted, I should hesitate to make any suggestion—except one: in the 'Epilogue,' Rebecca West tries to summarize her own book and fails—a warning for reviewers.

A description of that resplendent field cannot be attempted. Walking across it one can pick a few flowers (alas, picked flowers!) and gain certain impressions and conclusions. In some ways the book reminds me of Lawrence's *Seven Pillars of Wisdom*—even in its choice of title which is more happy than cogent, and not easy to explain. Both authors have a remarkable visual sense and the faculty of translating it into words; and both books have been lived, not merely written. Lawrence's style tends to over-elaboration, Rebecca West's is essentially natural, and often untidy. Her book necessarily lacks Lawrence's background of things done and suffered; but it throbs with life, and even with breathless excitement. It reminds me of Lawrence in the limpid beauty of its landscape-painting, in its rendering of the moods of men and nature, in the unified picture which

[1] Macmillan. 1942.
[2] Rebecca West is a great artist, and the above may be a rash judgment; the effect is perhaps deliberate.

emerges of country and people, and in the wisdom of a good many of its disquisitions. But it is unpremeditated in its sudden flashes of originality—which Lawrence never was.

When a reviewer claims to produce quotations 'well-nigh at random,' he has usually scanned the book, carefully tested various passages, tried them out in patterns, etc. It would be difficult, and hardly remunerative, to do that with Rebecca West's book: it does not pose for the reader or reviewer, it has no gems carefully mounted, and some of the best passages are spoilt by trivialities or slovenly writing. Its merit is in its totality, in which blemishes vanish and the human element conquers. I therefore forgo a hunt for quotations, and give a few from one chapter, on Macedonia, reproducing them in the order in which they occur.

Here is the description of a peasant woman in church at Easter:

> She was the age that all Macedonian women seem to become as soon as they cease to be girls: a weather-beaten fifty. There was a dark cloth about her hair and shoulders, and in its folds, and in her noble bones and pain-grooved flesh, she was like many Byzantine Madonnas to be seen in frescoes and mosaics. In her rough hand she mothered her taper, looking down on its flame as if it were a young living thing; and on the sleeve of her russet sheepskin jacket there showed an embroidery of stylized red and black trees which derived recognizably from a pattern designed for elegant Persian women two thousand years before. There was the miracle of Macedonia, made visible before our eyes.

> This woman had suffered more than most other human beings, she and her forebears. . . . But she had two possessions which any Western woman might envy. She had strength, the terrible stony strength of Macedonia . . .

and cupped in her destitution as in the hollow of a boulder there are the last drops of the Byzantine tradition.

That tradition survives in the Byzantine Church and in Byzantine art—'an art that is unique in its nobility . . . which makes all other arts seem a little naïve or gross.' Its

> achievements were not technical tricks but were signs of a real spiritual process, for the Byzantines were able to live in dignity and decency for four centuries in the knowledge that they were doomed, that one day they would be destroyed root and branch by the merciless Turks. They were not merely stoical in that shadow; they continued to live in the fullness of life, to create, even, in the very last phase of their doom. . . .

Then the invaders came: 'Asiatics as inaccessible to appeal as the personages in a nightmare.'

By now the flood of the invasion has long receded, but two distinct Moslem communities survive in Yugoslavia, one in Bosnia-Herzegovina and the other in Macedonia:

> Sarajevo is a Moslem, but not a Turkish town: a fantasia on Oriental themes worked out by a Slav population. Here in Skoplje we saw what the Oriental himself does with Oriental themes. Gone was the sense of form; we were faced with an essential discontinuity. . . .
>
> The Turks, I fancy, are a people who tire easily. When they are wildly excited, as they often are by militarist ardour and religious fanaticism, they cannot be fatigued; the reward for total abstinence from alcohol seems, illogically enough, to be the capacity for becoming intoxicated without it. But in ordinary life they seem subject to a languor that comes on in the day far too soon after dawn, and in a man's life far too soon after youth. The young Turk . . . after thirty-five . . . acquires a stolidity which might be mistaken for the outward sign of wisdom, were it not that it is impossible for so many to be in possession

of that rare quality. He is given to a gesture that claims to express deliberation, that is actually an indefinite postponement of thought. . . .

And how much there is in this simple description of a mosque:

> not an extraordinary building, save for the light cast on the cross-currents of Balkan culture by the contrast between its ancient and fine design and the white crudity of its substance.

Here is the description of an early iconostasis:

> This work is Byzantine in its recognition of the moral obligation to decorate, as extensively and intensively as possible, yet in its spirit it is purely peasant. When Abraham sets about sacrificing his son the boy stands in stockish obedience, as sons do in a good patriarchal society, and when the angel prevents him he looks up in exasperation like a farmer interrupted in a heavy job. . . .

And here are a few stray remarks or descriptions:

> . . . another song which they sang so slowly that to all intents and purposes it ceased to have a tune, but simply reserved the atmosphere for its melancholy.

> [A hotel manageress] one of those strange polyglots who seem to have been brought up in some alley where several civilizations put out their ash-cans.

> . . . the . . . town of Resan, which had the air characteristic of towns on southern plains, of having been pressed flat by the heavy thumb of the heat.

> . . . the lake, hyacinth-blue among mountains that were no colour at all, that were simply the colour of light which has met something hard and can go no further.

Here are two descriptions of females, culled from other chapters, which I cannot forgo reproducing—one of a woman who was plump as an elephant, but so beautiful that the resemblance only served to explain what it is that male elephants feel about female elephants. . . .

and the other of 'one of those widows whose majesty makes their husbands seem specially dead.'

Besides vision, art, and humour, there is in Rebecca West's book a great fund of knowledge—old, accumulated knowledge, or new, acquired in working on this book: for in it there is several years' labour extended over wide and varied regions.

3

'Yugoslavia is a necessity . . . not a predestined harmony.' What amazing uniformity there is in the vast expanse of Russia, a continent rather than a country! A Pole who travelled across Northern Russia recounts how, on waking up in the morning, he thought that the train had not moved all night, for he still saw the same birch forests. He might have added: also the same people. The traveller in England or France will, in a variety of scenery and types, apprehend a basic unity—it is rooted in modes of living and thinking, in a political régime common for centuries, in a common religion, in common memories, and most of all, in the final product, the consciousness of a common nationality. Even geographically Yugoslavia is, for her size, the most diversified of Slav countries: she has in Dalmatia a long coast and an old seafaring tradition; in Montenegro and Macedonia highland bastions, stark and formidable as in no other Slav land; in Croatia and the Banat oak forests and wheatfields, equal to any in the Slav plains. And what a variety there is of civilizations, religions, political memories, even of architecture! Yugoslavia lies half-way between Rome and 'Roum'—Byzantium, the Constantinople of the Greeks, the Tsargrad of the Slavs, the Istambul of the Turks. Roman Catholic in the West, Greek-Orthodox in the East, in the centre she harbours the only large body of Slav Moslems. The Adriatic coast was part of the Mediterranean world, Serbia and Macedonia of that of Byzantium, while Slovenia and Croatia experienced the influence of Central Europe. And yet, the peasant people has everywhere retained its Slav character and conscious-ness, which in the Greek Orthodox parts is strongly pro-Russian. (Here is an anecdote told by Rebecca West, which illustrates more than one point. A Montenegrin, asked how many there were of his people—and there are about 200,000—said: 'With Russia, 180 millions.' 'Yes, but how many without the Russians?' The Monte-negrin replied, 'We will never desert the Russians.')

Nature has made Yugoslavia 'a stage exquisitely set'; centuries have endowed her with a man-made heritage of beauty, unique in its variety; there is uncorrupted vigour of mind and body in her people. Why could not this diversity be woven into a rich pattern of national life and action, why is the intelligent, creative human animal so strangely self-destructive, practising 'perpetual cancellation' of his own achievements? Must there be this 'discrepancy between our lives and their framework,' this 'terrible complexity . . . in which nobody can be right and nobody can be wrong'? The Tower of Babel seems to be the lasting symbol of man's collective en-deavour. Rebecca West writes about Macedonia: 'there are few parts of the world that have known more politi-cally induced' [sorrows those who have laboured to build and plant, say, in East Galicia or in Palestine, can tell her that the number of countries which know as much is

growing]. This land . . . is astonishing in its beauty. . . .
Now a violet storm massed low on the far Albanian
mountains, and on the green plains at their feet walked
light'—not a ray but a cloud of light, unbounded yet
definite, 'a formless being which was very present, as
like God as anything we may see'; but the maintained
light walked over fields 'where hatreds are like poppies
among the corn.'

A hotel manager in the Dalmatian island of Hvar
railed at its people: '. . . they cultivate the tourist traffic
all summer, and talk politics all winter. Politics and
politics and politics, I am sick of politics. . . .'

> Such politics [writes Rebecca West in another connex-
> ion] are a leak in the community. Generous passion, pure
> art, abstract thought, run through it and are lost. There
> remain the obstinate solids which cannot be dissolved by
> argument or love, the rubble of hate and prejudice and
> malice, which are of no price . . . in Croatia I had from
> time to time felt very poor.

In Zagreb nothing mattered except 'the Croat-Serb
situation' which never seemed 'to get any further' amid
political disputation by intellectuals of the false sort
'that are always in opposition.' The Croats are spiritually
governed by the Roman Catholic Church, which 'owes
its tone to the Renaissance incorporated by Austria in
the Western bourgeois system'; they 'were experienced
in discomfort but not in tragedy.' The difference between
them and the Serbs at times seems to transcend racial
or linguistic unity.

This pervading, corroding influence of vague and
empty politics—Central-European politics—seems to
have paralysed Rebecca West when writing about
Croatia: there are fragments, but no unified picture.
Still, from personal experience I recognize in her failure

a true expression of the negative. But even Belgrade was to her 'a mournful city,' with a depressing air of anti-climax—'nothing real had happened here' of recent years. I saw Belgrade in the morning hours of a united Yugoslavia, she when a disappointing day was drawing to its close—again the failure of the artist is significant. The book is supreme in its descriptions of Dalmatia, Bosnia-Herzegovina, Macedonia, Old Serbia, and Monte-negro.

Each of the component Yugoslav countries is difficult to place anywhere except in a united Yugoslavia; yet it is equally difficult to solder their aggregate into one. In the centre of Dalmatia stands Split (Spoleto). Its old city nestles inside the palace which Diocletian, the greatest of Rome's Illyrian Emperors, built for himself after his abdication in A.D. 305. The houses are squeezed between the great Corinthian pillars, and almost one-fifth of Split's population still lives within the nine acres of the palace precincts. Along the Dalmatian coast and in the islands there are scores of towns, Slav counter-parts of the Italian cities, surrounded by walls and protected by forts, rich in palaces and churches—Gothic, Renaissance, or Baroque—each town with its distinct tradition. In the north, Senj was settled by Balkan Slavs, refugees from the Turks, who, as so many refugees, found all doors closed to them. Here they became a naval power, sea-rovers preying on the Turks: they perished when sold by Austria and Venice in a game of fraud and appeasement. Near it, upon an island, Rab is like so many Dalmatian towns: not much larger than a village, but the noble square in the centre, and the rich door-ways, windows, and columns of its houses, bespeak past magnificence. In the south, Dubrovnik (Ragusa) was for centuries a Slav republic ruled by a mercantile oligarchy;

fervently Roman Catholic though on the fringe of Greek Orthodox territory, it was favoured by the Papacy and Spain, remained independent of Venice and Turkey, and aloof from the other Slavs. It has great baroque churches and fine secular buildings—'an amazingly explicit town.' Trogir, near Split, on a minute island close to the coast, stands

> naked and leggy, for it is a walled city deprived of its walls. The Saracens levelled them, and the Venetians and the Hungarians would never let them be rebuilt. Now it looks like a plant grown in a flower-pot when the pot is broken but the earth and roots still hang together. On the quay stand Slavized Venetian palaces with haremish lattice-work fixed to screen the stone balconies, to show that here West meets East, brought thus far by Byzantine influence and perpetuated by the proximity of the Turks.

It was a Slav centre of the Manichaean creed; and in the porch to the bell-tower of its cathedral 'there is a carved portal which is the most massive and pure work of art produced by Manichaeism that I have ever seen.'

That creed, which had also a national character, struck deep roots in Bosnia. In 1415 its adherents, called Bogomils, condemned as heretics by both Rome and Byzantium, were offered by the Turks

> military protection, secure possession of their lands, and full liberty to practise their religion provided they counted themselves as Moslems and not as Christians, and did not attack the forces of the Ottoman Empire. The Bogomils, having been named in a Papal Bull with the Turks as common enemies of Christendom and having suffered invasion in consequence, naturally accepted the offer.

In time they changed into true Moslems, but retained the Slav language, and Sarajevo became the seat of a new Moslem nobility and the headquarters of the Bosnian Janissaries,

> a Free City in which the Slavs lived as they liked, according to a constitution they based on Slav law and custom, and defied all interference. It even passed a law by which the Pasha of Bosnia was forbidden to stay more than a night at a time within the city walls.

Alone among the Slavs they were partners, and not subjects, of the Ottoman Turks, and from Islam at its height took its luxury, militarism, and pride; and, above all, that 'love of pleasure . . . which was perhaps the greatest contribution the Turks had to make to culture.' From the hills surrounding Sarajevo one looks down on the minarets of a hundred mosques; in the town, costumes regarded 'as the distinguishing badge of an Oriental race . . . are worn by people far less Oriental in aspect than, say, the Latins; and this makes Sarajevo look like a fancy-dress ball.'

In Serb Macedonia, Byzantinism has survived in the churches and monasteries, in art and beliefs, in 'a culture which is not dominated by literature'; continued by people immured with their tradition. The growth of a Serb Byzantinism was cut short—but the stones of Ochrid, Bitolj, Skoplje, etc., still speak of the Tsars of the Nemanya dynasty, who in the thirteenth and fourteenth centuries founded the greatness of medieval Serbia. Their empire collapsed in 1389, when Tsar Lazar and his host were destroyed by the Turks in the Plain of Kossovo—a single battle sealed for five centuries the fate of the nation, condemning it to an existence which was 'not life but sheer nonsense,' to a 'night of evil' during which the pain of Kossovo was 'newly born in acuteness for each generation.'

In Old Serbia, the destruction of defeat was much more complete than in the mountains of Macedonia. But

> there stands on the Plain of Kossovo, some miles south of the actual battlefield, a building which demonstrates what sort of civilization fell with the Serbs . . . a chunk of the Nemanyan Empire, irrefutable testimony to its quality. We drove along the straight road, through low-spirited villages, past herds and flocks . . . slouching peasants, so few that the land was almost empty as the sky; and we turned into a lane leading towards the hills, through fields whose crops were smothered by those aromatic flowers which are half-way to being scrub. . . . Then, across a field of grey-green with the young maize, we saw a settlement of smallish farms lying among low trees, and in the midst of them a rose-red dome upheld by four lesser domes of the same warm and transparent colour. . . .
>
> Even from this distance it would be seen that Grachanitsa was as religious a building as Chartres Cathedral. . . . But it was as if Chartres Cathedral should stand alone on a land that has been shorn of all that was France when it was built and has been France since then. . . . Such spectacles are commonplace in Africa or Asia or America, which have their Pyramids and Angkor Vat and Inca memorials, but in Europe we are not accustomed to them. Our forms of historic tragedy have blotted a paragraph here and there, but they have rarely torn out the leaves of a whole volume, letting only a coloured frontispiece remain to tease us. Of Grachanitsa, however, catastrophe has left us nothing but Grachanitsa.

In that building lives the art, tradition, and history of the Serbs, and the memory of high culture and greatness—it is within the chapter on Grachanitsa that the account of the Nemanya Empire is rightly given by

Rebecca West. 'And when we went out of the church there was nothing.' Defeat had taken all.

Yet it was the defeated, suffering people of Serbia who conquered for Yugoslavia a new existence. The new freedom did not come from the one district which had remained free throughout the ages, from Montenegro—where 'sheer precipices and fretted peaks show the iron constitution our planet hides under its grass and flowers'; where the land is not barren, but is 'held in a cup of rock . . . insulated from the common tides of warmth that suffuses the rest of earth'; and where what the cup holds is pure, yet cold and dreary—'it is as if the genius of the place lacked emotional and intellectual pigmentation.' From the mountains of Macedonia where the Black Lamb is sacrificed on the blood-covered rock, and from the immensely sad plains of Serbia where the Grey Falcon forecast defeat, re-arose Yugoslavia.

In 1941–5 defeat and destruction were repeated, wrought once more by men as horrible 'as personages in a nightmare,' and so vile that (as Rebecca West says of an individual German) nobody who is not like them can believe how bad they are. But even after the German nightmare has passed away, the problem remains of how to transform the 'necessity' of Yugoslavia into a 'harmony.'

5

POLAND

THE DESTINY of nations is written on the globe. The English Channel and the vast Eurasian spaces have placed Britain and Russia beyond the reach of Europe and enabled them to check and destroy its would-be world conquerors. The geographical configuration of Spain, France, and Italy has provided frameworks so distinct and permanent as to make these nation-States appear preordained: when the curtain rises they are seen like Adam in an Elizabethan morality play crossing the stage on their way to be created. The centrifugal configuration of Germany favoured expansion but impeded unity; there is no focal district or capital to bind together the three Germanies of the Rhine, the Danube, and the Northern Plain. The Poles were the first of the Slavs to withstand the impact of the German advance to the East in the open plain ('pola' in the Slav languages means 'fields,' and the 'Polak' is their inhabitant). In the south the Carpathians form Poland's frontier, and in the north the Baltic; the Vistula, from its sources in Silesia to its delta at Danzig, is her backbone; but there is nothing to demarcate her frontiers west or east: Poland lacks both shape and expanse—she stands penultimate in the European chain of nations, for Russia intervenes between her and the only *Lebensraum*, contiguous to Europe, where unimpeded growth is possible.

At first 'the Russias' were an inchoate mass, prey for conquering neighbours: till a hard core developed and a centre arose in Moscow, at the portages between the Western Dvina, the Dnieper, and the Volga, whence the 'gathering of the Russian lands' started, north, west, and south, and a rapid colonization to the east. The Poles, as a people, were at all times inferior in numbers to the Germans and the Russians; but while these were divided or distracted, they made a bid for national greatness which at one time seemed near succeeding: three centuries ago the Polish State had, barring France, the largest population and, barring Russia, the largest territory in Europe. But when the tide turned and failure ensued there was no hard shell into which Poland could withdraw (as did Sweden, Spain, and France), and she suffered obliteration, still retaining assets left over from the attempt which had miscarried, and claims based on those assets. The difficulties of her frontiers with the two most numerous nations of Europe were thus aggravated, making the Polish question a crucial and excruciating problem of international politics. 'Que voulez-vous, mon ami,' said M. Briand to Sir Austen Chamberlain at a time when Europe seemed otherwise to be settling down to an ordered existence, 'la Pologne c'est le rheumatisme de l'Europe.'

The rise and fall of Yagellon Poland is the story of her bid for greatness. In the fourteenth century the gradual withdrawal of the Poles in the west and advance against the east were completed with a jerk; Pomerania and Silesia were given up, Halich 'Russ' (the modern East Galicia) was acquired, and, most important of all, Poland entered into a dynastic union with the Lithuania of the Yagellons. This was no longer what its name would suggest: Russian was the language, and Greek Orthodoxy the religion, of the great majority of its population, and during the next 250 years it competed with Moscow for the leadership of 'all the Russias.' The upper strata of society in those wide territories, extending from Brest-Litovsk to Smolensk, and from Przemysl beyond Kiev, preferred, on the whole, to share the rights and freedoms which the Polish 'gentry-Republic' offered to its privileged classes, rather than submit to the fierce despotism of Moscow's rulers. But there were qualms and misgivings, and strenuous endeavours on the part of the Russian gentry to preserve its national identity and religion. Yet by the force of circumstances, and mostly without compulsion, a process of denationalization occurred, on a scale unequalled anywhere in Europe. The peculiar character of the gentry-Republic facilitated the transition, and was in turn accentuated by it; no unity of the vernacular was required, for Latin was the language of the Polish State, of its legislature and legislation; nor of race—besides the Lithuanian, White Russian, and Ukrainian magnates and gentry, smaller bodies of German nobles, and even a few exotic groups (of Moslem Tartars, Armenians, and Jewish converts) were received and merged into the gentry-nation. Nor was any attempt made at first to establish uniformity of religion—possibly such latitudinarianism at a time when religion supplied the tie of nationality was a corollary of the non-national character of a commonwealth based on caste. The Polish Protestants, even while very numerous and zealous, failed to develop their own form of national religion; but Reformation and Counter-Reformation alike helped to weld the gentry of the entire Republic into one coherent community—many of the leading families effected the transition from the Eastern Church to Rome via Protestantism. There was one great proselytizing effort turned to a political purpose: union with Rome was to sever the bond which connected the Greek Orthodox population of Poland and Lithuania with Moscow. Most of the higher clergy and of the upper classes eventually accepted this implication of their political connexion with Poland, while the peasant masses, hostile to the big landowners, to Poland and Rome, finally rose in social, national, and religious revolt.

Had the Uniat Church taken firm root among the White and Little Russians (or 'Ukrainians'), the separation of these western branches of 'Russ' from Great Russia would have been clear and final; and to break up their national and religious unity has for centuries been a foremost aim of Polish policy and endeavours. This has probably been the chief source of hostility between Russia and Poland. But even where the Poles succeeded in implanting the seeds of an anti-Russian separatism, they themselves reaped the harvest of bitter hostility from peasant nationalisms. The Polonized upper classes in the 'borderlands' burdened Poland with a heritage of conflicts and contradictions which for a second time proved fatal to her in the period of 1918–39.

Muscovite Russia was at all times a despotism making its appeal to the masses (which does not preclude ferocious repressions); and the less consciousness there was of political rights in those capable of exercising them, the more religion supplied an (essentially democratic) criterion of community and allegiance. At the time of the Partitions of Poland no one, in determining the nationality of a country, would have taken account of the language spoken by peasant-serfs, while of the Polish gentry-Republic, the districts, say, of Vitebsk or Kiev were as much part as those round Poznań or Cracow; but the Eastern Church was Russia's criterion. In terms of the 'political nation' as then constituted, her share in the Partitions was no less culpable than that of Prussia or

Austria when these annexed Poznań and Warsaw, Cracow and Lublin; but to-day Russia's gains are seen to have stretched nowhere beyond the Curzon Line. It was by way of the Napoleonic Duchy of Warsaw (composed of territories recovered from Prussia and Austria) and the 'Congress' Kingdom of 1815 that Polish ethnic territories came to be joined to Russia; and Poles who favoured such dynastic union under the Tsar—foremost among them was Alexander I's friend, Prince Adam Czartoryski—hoped that it would lead to an ultimate re-union with the provinces lost to Russia in the Partitions.

In time the world forgot which territories Russia had acquired in the Partitions and which under a European 'mandate,' and all her dealings with the Poles were seen in the light of the cruel wrongs and persecutions inflicted upon them. Nor was it possible for the Poles during the period of political extinction to modernize their ideas of what was their rightful national heritage; but when Poland re-arose, they had to recognize that Russia could not be relegated to the frontier of 1772—unless, in a gamble for a new 'Yagellon' federation, the Poles themselves were prepared to cede the territories east of the Curzon Line to Lithuania, White Russia, and the Ukraine. After some initial hesitations they preferred to bite off as much as they thought they could digest and, in drawing the Riga Line, left Russia her gains from the first two Partitions (without this visibly affecting the language used by historians or politicians about Russia's part in them). As for the territories between the Curzon and the Riga Lines, the Poles would argue that anyhow these were no concern of Moscow, for they were White Russian and Ukrainian; and to the end they failed to make up their minds whether to 'share' (or shall we say 'partition'?) White Russia and the Ukraine with Great

Russia, or to play them off against her. They finished by attempting both: a hopeless farrago.

In the east a Polonized gentry covered extensive non-Polish territories; in the west large districts, especially in East Prussia and Silesia, inhabited by Polish peasants and workmen, had lost their upper classes and towns to the Germans—the 'jerk' in the fourteenth century produced two pictures on one photographic plate. An integral resetting of Poland was one of the preconditions of peace in Eastern and Central Europe.

The time of Poland's bondage, by precluding normal development, has left behind a heavy burden of intellectual maladjustment: historical and political conceptions hardened, and, divorced from reality, tended to change into *clichés* or fantasies. Polish thought was subordinated to the purpose of national restoration: it could not afford to be objective. There was egocentrism and exaltation, self-righteousness and self-castigation, and—above all— boundless heroism and devotion (it is easier for the sick and the wronged to attain sainthood than to preserve a sense of proportion). W. Mickiewicz, the son of the poet, wrote in 1870: 'Il n'est pas plus possible de faire de la bonne politique sans la Pologne que de rêver une pure morale sans Dieu.' Lechon, one of Poland's best poets of the inter-war period, exclaimed with relief after she had re-arisen: 'Spring has come to the world, let me behold the spring and not Poland.' But for Polish historians and political writers there was to be no such release from pragmatic obsessions, or 'national duty.'

The wholly abnormal conditions of 1918—the coincident effacement of Germany and Russia—brought to life the double personality on the photographic plate: against two neighbours, either potentially far more powerful than Poland, she was able to enforce mutually contradictory claims. In the west these were based on the democratic principle, in the east on the historic heritage of the upper classes—thus, for instance, every argument which supported Poland's claims to Upper Silesia, destroyed, even more thoroughly, her converse claim to East Galicia. A proverb says that you can sit on one stool only—'but we sit on a whole collection of furniture,' confessed to me a distinguished Pole some twenty years ago. The position was politically unsound and intellectually demoralizing. The Poles had flouted the verdict of the Allies, by which they had promised to abide, and had, in drawing for themselves the Riga Line, doubled their territory; and even in their methods had shown scant regard for propriety in international relations (Zeligowski's 'rebellion' is their best-known exploit of that kind). But having got themselves into a dangerous predicament they appealed to the world's conscience to sanction their performances and to guarantee their gains —of these the justice had therefore to be proved, and also the ignorance or bad will of anyone who thought otherwise. In a frantic yet sustained campaign of self-deception and propaganda, facts and arguments were twisted, and statistics were faked; and every treatise, be it about the proverbial elephant, led up to a vindication of Poland's right to Vilna and Lvov (and to anything else which had been put into the bag with them). When the present tragedy supervened, an intellectual pea-soup fog precluded sane and sober reorientation.

Can this be achieved now, late in the day? Occasionally signs of honest self-criticism are discernible in pamphlets and articles printed in Polish; practically never in foreign-language publications. It is extremely difficult for Poles, at a time like the present, to speak out before a foreign public: oblivious of the use, or abuse,

which may be made of their admissions, and indifferent
to the anger of their own countrymen (Mr. Chamberlain,
when trying to silence critics of Munich, talked, with
much less excuse, about 'fouling one's own nest').
Cromwell ordered the painter to paint him 'warts and
all'; Queen Elizabeth forbade even a single shadow in
her portrait; but the pictures of Poland, mostly by inferior artists, are not like that uncanny image of the great
Queen—much more like faces which 'pleasingly' smile
at the camera. There is beauty, grandeur, and pathos in
Poland's history: in the history of that gentry-Republic
whose constitutional development deserves a thorough
comparative analysis; in the history of its descendants,
revolutionary knights-errant, social amphibians, aristocrats who, about the middle of the nineteenth century,
became the 'General Staff of the world's *sans-culottes*'
(Balzac wrote about one of that type: 'il s'est battu
comme un Polonais, comme un patriote, comme un
homme qui n'a rien: trois raisons pour se bien battre');
in the history of patient workers who, after every disaster,
sought national recovery in 'organic labour.' There is
intense interest in the interplay of different conceptions
of the 'political nation'; of nationality, territorial and
linguistic; and in the part which Poland has played in
international affairs, and foreign Powers in Polish history. But to do full justice to all concerned, and to draw
the inexorable conclusions, dispassionate aloofness is
required, and a singleminded pursuit of the truth: which,
perhaps, it is too much to expect in days of pain, sorrow,
and anger.

Of foreigners, on the other hand, few know Polish,
and hardly any are capable of fathoming the depths and
of unravelling the complexities of Polish problems.
Even the best-trained among them are liable to come

croppers (like a London hostess who had Highland pipers for the wedding feast of a Lowland couple). Moreover, some are devotees worshipping at the shrine of 'martyred Poland' (a laudable attitude, but unprofitable in a historian), and some, embarrassed by the tragedy, mince words and mumble (history-writing is not a visit of condolence). And so book after book published about Poland proves unhelpful, unenlightening, and unconvincing.

A new collective work on Poland[1] has appeared under distinguished auspices, in a series which aims at presenting 'an honest, sincere, and objective appraisal of the United Nations.' The volume was planned and its contributors were selected by Professor Bernadotte E. Schmitt (one of the foremost authorities on European diplomatic history) in consultation with the general editor of the series, Professor Robert J. Kerner (a well-known expert on East-European history), on whom most of the editorial work devolved when, in 1943, Professor Schmitt 'entered upon some special work.' In a brilliant editor's preface, Professor Schmitt speaks about the '"case study" for political scientists' provided by the Poland of 1919–39, the progress she had achieved, and her ultimate failure.

In the perspective of twenty-five years, it now seems clear that the high hopes of 1919 were defeated by three circumstances. In the first place, Poland failed to devise a satisfactory foreign policy. Lying between Germany and Russia . . . Poland tried to play one off against the other but succeeded only in uniting them against itself. Secondly, the Polish Government failed to satisfy the

[1] *Poland.* Edited by Bernadotte E. Schmitt. (The United Nations Series.) University of California Press. London: Cambridge University Press. 1945.

national minorities which comprised nearly one-third of
the population. . . . Thirdly, the democratic political
régime . . . was gradually replaced by a semi-dictator-
ship. . . .

A very sound diagnosis: but not followed up by an
inquiry into the origin of this triple failure. It was obvious
from the outset that Germany would not be reconciled
to the loss of her eastern provinces: therefore, by acquir-
ing territory with over 7,000,000 White Russians and
Ukrainians, Poland condemned herself, in her foreign
policy, to a non-stop acrobatic performance of balancing
between Germany and Russia; and only exceptional
conditions enabled her to continue it so long. Secondly,
no government could have satisfied 'national minorities'
which comprised not 'nearly,' but considerably more
than, one-third of the total population, and formed, in
fact, the majority in about one-half of the country.
Thirdly, a State so circumstanced and constituted was
bound to seek precarious security in a military dictator-
ship. Geography and history have combined in setting
an exceedingly difficult task to the Poles, and before 1945
little had been done to simplify it.

Editing a collective work demands great skill, knowledge, and application: bone must be gathered to his
bone, and breath enter the body. It adds to the difficulties when the contributors are of different nationalities: though in this case the better factual knowledge of
the Poles and the greater objectivity of the Americans,
if properly used, might have served as a mutual corrective. But no such technique seems to have been applied:
or so basic a problem as the national composition of
Poland's population before the war would have been properly examined: and then Professor Schmitt would
hardly quote, even with an obvious reservation, that in

1919, 'according to Polish sources,' 42 per cent in East Galicia were Polish, or Mr. Roucek, with a similar reservation, that in 1931 only 51·9 per cent were Ukrainian (in 1910 the respective figures had been 23 and 64, and could not have changed to that extent, except on paper). Nor does the book seem as a whole to have been critically revised; one contributor puts the gentry in the old Polish Republic at almost 10 per cent of the population, another at around 15, and a third at nearly 12 (see pp. 44, 219, and 334): and all three omit to name the date, and therefore the territory, to which their estimates refer. Or again, one contributor says that 'before leaving Poland, President Mościcki appointed Wladyslaw Raczkiewicz as his successor,' while another gives the date of 30th September 1939, that is, about a fortnight after Mościcki had arrived in Rumania—and a great deal turns on the circumstances of that transaction.

No one would question the fine qualities and heroic deeds of the Poles, but the blaring self-glorification of some of these essays is bound to evoke a critical reaction. This is how propaganda should not be made, and history must not be written, and the editor would have done service to Poland's cause by toning down such passages. Self-praise is accompanied by occasional depreciation of others and by indiscriminate indictments of the Partitioning Powers; but even with regard to their deeds, or misdeeds, a modicum of historical accuracy is desirable. Lord Dupplin wrote to the Duke of Newcastle from Lisbon in 1759 that the absence of anything that was lacking—beautiful churches, fine pictures, or virginity— was ascribed to the earthquake; so in these Polish essays the loss of anything, even if it is not missing, is charged against the Partitioning Powers. 'More than one hundred years of political terror and economic exploitation by the

three Partitioning Powers . . .' is the *leit-motif* of the
Polish writers. Great was the disaster of 1755, and terrible
the wrong of political extinction—but why exaggerate?
There was no 'political terror' under Prussia; nor under
Russia before 1830; and during the last fifty years under
Austria the government of both Polish and Ukrainian
Galicia was in Polish hands.

> All three parts of Poland [writes M. H. Zielinski] were
> in a deplorable state of economic backwardness, for it had
> been the policy of the Partitioning Powers to keep Polish
> lands from participating in the tremendous economic and
> technical progress of the nineteenth century. . . . The
> exclusion of Polish territories from the epoch-making
> progress of industrialization . . .

Embedded in this letterpress appears a map of disrupted
Poland, including Upper Silesia, one of the most highly
industrialized regions in Europe; and a different essayist,
in the next chapter, remarks that 'after the restoration of
Poland's independence, it became apparent that some
of its industries had been overdeveloped,' having hitherto produced for the vast Russian markets. None of the
Polish contributors has a kind word for the Habsburg
Monarchy. One of them talks about 'the flame of
national spirit which was in danger of being quenched
by the policy of extermination of the three Partitioning
Powers—Russia, Prussia, and Austria'; another of
Poland 'prostrate under the heels of three empires for
five generations' and the Poles unable 'to express themselves in self-government'; a third says that 'of the three
hostile governments . . . only one, namely the Austrian,
had maintained a system of compulsory Polish schools,'
and that 'not one of the three occupants of Poland had
spent much money on school buildings' (but in Galicia
schools and school buildings were the concern of the

autonomous Polish authorities, and Professor Orvis is unduly hard on them when describing it as a region 'without railways or schools'); and a fourth merely says that Austria's 'policies toward a number of the nationalities were somewhat liberal. . . .' But whatever may have been the motives of the Habsburgs—Catholic or aristocratic sympathies, dynastic calculations, a common hostility to Russia, need of Polish support in the Vienna Parliament—the fact remains that during fifty years before the First World War the Poles ranked high in their favour, and that during that war both the dynasty and a majority of the Galician Poles wished for 'the Austrian Solution of the Polish Question' (a union of Galicia with Russian Poland under the Habsburgs). Why thus wipe out a chapter of Polish history—in which the Poles learnt and achieved a great deal? The Cracow Conservatives (the so-called *Stańczyki*) were one of the most cultured political groups which Poland ever produced, her enlightened Tories.

6

RUSSIA

[THE FIRST three of the essays comprised under this heading appeared in *The Times* on 10 March 1943 and on 14 and 15 January 1944, and I reproduce them unchanged; I even eschew alterations which I otherwise should have made to avoid repeating certain points from the preceding essay. The form of these articles reflects the time of their publication; but the underlying contentions seem to me as valid now as they were then.

World Empires blend power instincts with a measure of isolationism; and the resultant is a 'sphere of interests.' It is sound policy in such Empires not to interfere unless they can, and mean to, do so effectively; the greater the power, the greater should be the sense of responsibility. At all times it is therefore necessary 'to weigh interests and measure distances': once more the resultant is a sphere of interests. The obvious basis for a settlement between World Empires is a delimitation of such spheres; but a hazy 'internationalism,' the hangover of nineteenth-century liberalism and League of Nations doctrines, has led, even in the present post-war period, to indiscriminate irresponsible meddling. The Soviets, from their own Communist angle, are inclined that way —the more important was it from the outset to try to attain a settlement with them on the basis of spheres of interest, which, judging by the restraint shown by them during the original troubles in Greece, they would have been willing to accept. This was not done; and a point may be reached when both sides will have engaged too far to revert to what would have been the only feasible and sensible basis of agreement. To play the 'liberal' missionary to the world is rather *vieux jeu*, and moreover beyond the present strength and means of this country.

Of the Polish problem, which in the past has caused much international meddling, and which is the subject of the second and third of these essays, these seem the basic facts:

1. A 're-setting' of Poland had to be achieved through a withdrawal of scattered Polish minorities in the east, and a consolidation of Poland's territory, cleared of Germans, in the west. An end had to be put to a situation bound to recreate, again and again, a Russian–German alliance. To live, Poland had to be made 'fair and square,' with the Curzon line for her eastern border, a similar straight line in the west, and a broad frontage on the Baltic; and with no Polish enclaves outside, or alien enclaves inside, Poland.

2. Whether it was necessary to extend Poland's territory to the Oder and Neisse, or whether East Prussia, Danzig, and an undivided Upper Silesia, would have sufficed, it is too late to discuss now. The matter was decided at Potsdam: and it is no good pleading the 'provisional' character of that decision which may have satisfied a cheap taste for outward appearances—it would have been more honest and more humane to have made the settlement final. For then the modes of removing the Germans might have been settled with the Poles, whereas the 'provisional' settlement well-nigh forced them to create a *fait accompli* at any cost and with the least possible delay.

3. This has now been created. To question it can

merely make difficulties for the Poles (and it is not for this country to add to their sufferings), and evoke hopes and desires in the Germans which the Anglo-Saxon Powers cannot satisfy. But the Soviets could do so at any moment—at the expense of Poland and as the price of a new Russian–German alliance. The Anglo-Saxon Powers may possibly be able to nurse Germany back to strength and appetite: but Russia, whenever so inclined, will be able to outbid them with Germany, as Germany was able to outbid the Western Powers with Russia in 1939. A Russian–German alliance would dominate the European continent, and a great deal besides; and it now depends on Russia whether it is re-created. Such an alliance is supremely dangerous to the world, has in practice proved invariably disastrous for Russia, and deadly for Poland. A sensible delimitation of spheres of interest would serve a much better purpose than the pointless wrangles to which we are now treated at every international conference.

4. The Anglo-Saxon Powers cannot reach Poland with a view to increasing, maintaining, or reducing her territory, or even to securing her real independence, however desirable this might be. Therefore, the less they interfere where they cannot act, and do not mean to, the better for all concerned.]

(1) BRITAIN, RUSSIA, AND EUROPE

DOES IT occur to American isolationists how English they are in their deep instinctive dislike of European entanglements and commitments? The Tory country gentlemen readily renounced the fruits of Marlborough's victories: they were weary of the Continent, and wished to be rid of it. The 'wretched Electorate' of Hanover long remained a sore in British politics, and a reproach: it was a link with the Continent; its welcome loss favourably reacted on the position of the dynasty in this country. In the nineteenth century Continental alliances were shunned, and no policy could have been more English and more popular than 'splendid isolation.' The nation's energy and resources were not to be frittered away in unprofitable Continental squabbles.

This, in fact, is the natural attitude of a nation intent on developing an empire or a continent of its own. It is shared by America and by the great Empire of Russia, which in essence transcends Europe, and which over its inner development or Asiatic expansion is apt, at times, to forget even the Balkans, although to Russia, for a number of reasons, this is the most interesting region in Europe. No nation deeply engaged on the European continent has managed to develop or retain wide extra-European territories; and no nation engaged in developing such territories willingly lets itself be drawn into Continental affairs. (But what we call Continental, Americans call European, and this island being a link and transmitter between Europe and North America, the dislike of European entanglements is liable to receive an anti-British colouring.) Indeed the spiritual insularity of this country goes deeper than the professed ignorance of American isolationists who have much of the European continent in their midst. And as for the man of Kazan, he is far more remote from Europe than the man of Kansas.

There is a tradition of spiritual unity in Europe, deriving from Rome. But whenever in the last three centuries a nation or dynasty tried to re-create this politically, by establishing its own predominance over Western Christendom, it met with the conscious and tenacious resistance of England; and in defeating these threats to her own freedom and independence, England has gained about half of White Man's Land outside Europe for her language, culture, and tradition. Had Philip II of Spain been victorious, no English-speaking communities would have arisen in America. Had the Bourbons prevailed, New England and Virginia might have succumbed to Quebec and Louisiana, as New Amsterdam had to the English colonies. But so decisive was by 1806 Britain's naval superiority that the United States did not have to consider how the Napoleonic Empire would affect her own further development. In this century the German menace has placed Britain's frontier on the Rhine, and America's at Dover: there are times when honest isolationists have to overcome their cherished (and well-founded) dislikes.

Neither for good nor for evil has Europe ever been able to form a free union: not even against the conquering Turk, when religion and the common tradition seemed most to demand it. European co-operation can sometimes be achieved through a concert of the Great Powers exercising a temperate measure of control. But integral European union would require coercion. Before 1795 attempts at universal dominion were unsuccessful, for there was a fair balance between the contending systems. In 1810, for the first time, the entire European continent, from the Channel Ports to the frontiers of Russia, was under one ruler. Even so, potential centres of independent strength endured on the Continent, and in 1813–15 the two Germanic Powers played a part hardly inferior to that of Great Britain and Russia. In 1914–18 French resistance was of supreme importance; still, it was the joint weight of Russia and the two English-speaking empires which accomplished Germany's defeat; the balance of population and power had already shifted to a marked degree against the purely European nations, and in favour of the extra-European empires. But Russia's collapse, in the years 1917–20, was unfortunately allowed to obscure her past performance and her future importance, while the pacifist isolationism of the Anglo-Saxons well-nigh eliminated their influence from the European continent.

After 1922 France, much inferior in her power-potential to any of the three empires, as also to Germany, had the Continent to herself—a weight far beyond her strength to carry; and the system into which she now glided, during Russia's temporary eclipse, recalled that which had existed before Russia emerged as a Great Power. In the seventeenth century Sweden, Poland, and Turkey were France's eastern counterpoise to the Greater Germany of the Habsburgs; but they changed into a liability when, under Peter the Great, Russia entered the European arena and engaged in conflict with the three. And when in the second half of the eighteenth century the two Germanic Powers joined hands with Russia, France withdrew; distant and single-handed she could not be effective. Napoleon's victories carried him into Eastern Europe—to his own destruction. He succumbed in the conflict with Russia, which he had tried his best to avoid. Experience proves, most emphatically, that no Western Power, however great, can safely act on the eastern flank of Germany except in a genuine and close understanding with Russia.

The Continental nations, hopelessly divided, are no match for Germany, especially if she manages to enlist the sympathy of one of the three extra-European white empires. The League of Nations was to have supplied the framework of a peace system—but who was to work it? Russia, defeated and Bolshevist, and estranged from her allies, was abandoned by them and mutilated by her neighbours; the United States withdrew from Europe; France, with an unresisting automatism, lapsed into that system from which, during the preceding 200 years, even in the days of her prepotency, she had consciously recoiled; and Great Britain, realizing the folly of the French system, tried to limit her commitments to Western Europe, as if international affairs, involving the balance of power on the Continent, could be transacted in water-tight compartments.

Naturally every State tried to use the League of Nations for its own policies and purposes: France and her satellites, to collect a maximum of 'binding' guarantees for the frontiers drawn by them in 1919 and 1920; Germany, to re-enter the concert of Europe as one of the Great Powers; Russia, to construct a system of collective security against the Nazis who noisily paraded their anti-Russian designs. Great Britain's purpose in the League was innocent and pathetic: to look wise and virtuous without much exertion—to attain the unbought ease of life. The British were pacifists and isolationists— there is affinity between the desire for peace and the wish to be left alone. To escape Continental entanglements they went into the League of Nations—a paradoxical pursuit—and many a distinguished British champion of the League felt, deep down in his heart, how beautiful it would be were there no foreigners in it! Moreover, Parliamentary forms in League transactions were apt to reassure and mislead Englishmen—people seldom inquire how things work with which they have been familiar all their lives. On the Parliamentary analogy, an efficacy was subconsciously ascribed to votes and verdicts of Council and Assembly which could not have been reasonably asserted.

The shams, illusions, and neglects of the twenty years 1919–39 must not be reproduced after this war. If rest is to come to Europe, and a period of peaceful and productive development to the very much wider White Man's lands outside, if an end is now to be made of the German menace and Europe is to be resettled on a lasting basis, this basis must be sought in an association between the three great extra-European empires and European nations which seek peace and not adventure; but the necessary antecedent to regional arrangements is a truly close collaboration between the three empires. Disunion between them, and their withdrawal from Europe, annulled the victory of 1918.

(2) RUSSIA AND POLAND

During the last 150 years, the relation of Russia to Prussia tended to determine the pattern of international politics on the Continent, more so than was realized in periods which overrated the power and importance of France and Austria. This relation, in turn, was greatly affected by the Polish question. Polish claims against Prussia and Russia, whether equitable or exaggerated, fostered a community of interests between the two which any threat of outside intervention was apt to convert into active partnership. Napoleon, to rivet down the Continent from both ends, persistently sought an alliance with Russia, and avoided sponsoring the Polish cause, though at that time the two Germanic Powers alone held truly Polish land. But in wide Russian provinces, extending from Brest-Litovsk to Vitebsk and Kiev, while the peasantry was overwhelmingly White Russian or Ukrainian, the land-owning classes were Polonized or Polish; and what counted then was the nationality of the masters, not of their serfs. The name of Poland had therefore very wide connotations. When circumstances made Napoleon form Polish territories recovered from Prussia and Austria into an independent State, he called it the Duchy of Warsaw, and refused to assume its government or to give it to one of his family, but twice offered it to Tsar Alexander. Dynastic union was then what 'federation' is now. Napoleon realized that a Russian-Polish *bloc* on Germany's eastern flank could play in with France, while a union of Poland with France would produce a Russian-Prussian *entente*.

Poland carries a grievous burden in her geographical contours and historical heritage. In the west, her vital and indefeasible ethnic claims lacerate the body of Prussia; in the east, memories and traditions, and doubtful and dwindling assets inherited from the old republic, embroil her with the White Russians and the Ukrainians, and through them with Russia. Polish sway over those vast eastern territories resembled the 'Protestant ascendancy' in Southern Ireland, and was equally untenable; but a century of political submersion rendered it infinitely more difficult for the Poles to comprehend the change which the rise of the masses to political life was producing in the national character of those territories. Moreover, the Polish gentry in those eastern borderlands were a far more numerous class than, for instance, the German barons in the Baltic provinces or the Anglo-Irish landed gentry; they were neither conquerors nor intruders but mostly as autochthonous as the peasantries, from whom they had become estranged in language and religion by a gradual process of cultural absorption into the gentry-Republic. To this day the core of the Polish educated classes is of gentry extraction, while even those who are not have been brought up in its traditions;

and within their ranks the eastern 'borderers' were for a long time pre-eminent through their numbers, wealth, and achievements. As they supplied a large proportion of Poland's political and intellectual leaders (Pilsudski was their last outstanding exponent), their traditional claims ranked high and continued to be pressed, thus rendering collaboration with Russia impossible.

In the eighteenth century there was among the Poles a Prussian and a Russian 'orientation,' both parties recognizing that support from one of the two neighbours was indispensable. In 1815 the 'Congress' Kingdom of Poland was formed in dynastic union with Russia. It was the work of Alexander I and of his Polish friend, Prince Adam Czartoryski, not of Russian statesmen: the Poles hoped, and the Russians feared, that it would lead to an inclusion in the Polish State of the 'alienated provinces' in the east. The ill-assorted partnership of these two nations, initiated at the Vienna Congress, for a hundred years poisoned the political life of both.

During the century 1815–1918 two political types competed for leadership among the Poles: the 'realist' adherents of compromise and the romantic revolutionaries; the sober Conservatives and the imaginative Radicals; the Whites and the Reds. Compromise meant working with either Russia or with the Habsburg Monarchy which, being Roman Catholic and multinational, was obviously preferable to Prussia as an ally. Radicalism, from 1789 onwards, pinned its hopes on France, on Western Europe, or on European revolution. France spoke with two voices. Thus, in 1830, La Fayette declared: 'All France is Polish'; Louis-Philippe protested: 'It is necessary to weigh interests and measure distances'; and his Premier, Casimir Périer: 'Nothing but the interest of France can make us fight . . . the blood of Frenchmen belongs to France alone.' But the Poles, fearless fighters and visionary politicians, were apt to accuse their own 'moderates' of faintheartedness, and to look upon strangers who tried to bring them down to earth as enemies.

In 1914 the outbreak of war between the Partitioning Powers produced two Polish 'compromise' schemes: on the side of the Central Powers, for a union of Russian and Austrian Poland under the Habsburgs, including East Galicia and possibly some other eastern border-lands, but not Prussian Poland; on the Russian side, for a union of all ethnic Polish territory, including Prussian Poland, but without East Galicia or any other extension in the east. Pilsudski and his group of national revolu-tionaries started on the side of the Central Powers, but renounced nothing; and through a most extraordinary combination of events their dreams came true. All the three Partitioning Powers collapsed, and Poland re-arose in a void. It seemed no longer necessary 'to weigh in-terests and measure distances.' But while the incredible can be achieved at a juncture, can it be made to last?

Pilsudski planned to break up Russia, and to re-create a 'Yagellon' union with an 'independent' Ukraine and White Russia (and also with Lithuania). The scheme was impracticable: anti-Russian separatism was almost non-existent outside East Galicia; moreover, a deep social gulf divided the peasantries of the borderlands from the Poles. In opposition to Pilsudski, the former 'moderates' developed a programme of unrealistic realism and un-idealistic utopianism. At Riga Poland demanded and obtained as much White Russian and Ukrainian terri-tory as she thought she would be able to assimilate integrally, and ever since has claimed this to be a supreme piece of moderation. Dmowski talked about a 'Great

Power' Poland as a 'barrier' between Germany and Russia, and an outpost of Western Europe against both; and he found considerable support in France. But how long could such a barrier have held out against the joint forces of those two neighbours? As Germany and Russia began to recover, the policy of France became uneasy and uncertain, while that of Poland changed into break-neck tight-rope dancing. To drive Russia into partner-ship with Germany spells disaster for the rest of Europe —and, in the long run, for Russia herself.

In 1863 Napoleon III's half-hearted and ineffective *démarche* on behalf of Poland played into the hands of Bismarck who took the side of Russia and received his reward in 1866 and 1870. Had Bismarck's policy been continued, neither an isolated and weakening France nor the Anglo-Saxon countries, anyhow loath to emerge from their isolation, would have been a counterpoise to the three empires of Eastern and Central Europe. The folly of William II gave rise to the Triple Entente. The folly of the Franco-Polish system of 1921, which tried both to encircle Germany and to draw a *cordon sanitaire* round Russia, re-created an understanding between the two. This was broken by Hitler's advent. Russia entered the League of Nations and was ready to co-operate with Western Europe and Poland against Nazi Germany; for a while France, under Barthou, the last of the Triple Entente statesmen, was willing to join hands with Russia. But not so Pilsudski or his epigoni. During the Munich period, and even to some extent after Prague, Russia was cold-shouldered by the Western Powers; once more a Russian-German agreement was concluded. And for a third time Germany destroyed her own chances—by prematurely attacking Russia.

A Russian priest once tried to prove to a doubting

peasant that miracles do occur—by presuming their occurrence: 'Were I to jump from this tower,' he said, 'and land safely, what would you call it?' 'An accident,' replied the peasant. 'And if I did it a second time?' 'Another accident.' 'And a third time?' 'A habit.' Three times 'accidents' have saved the world from German dominion: but would it be reasonable to assume that doing so has become fate's habit? The friendship of Russia enabled Bismarck to erect the mighty edifice of the Second Reich; the estrangement between the Western Powers and Russia enabled Hitler and his Third Reich to attain predominance in Europe. But German predominance is at least as dangerous to Russia as to the West: for, while the Germans try to vanquish the West, they are out to conquer and acquire the East of Europe, the traditional 'space' for their 'colonization.' It is in the vital interest of both Poland and Russia, and, indeed, of all Europe, that the old Russian-Polish feud should now be settled for good and all. Such a settlement between Russia and Poland would best be secured by a frontier which either way left no substantial bodies of men on the wrong side; this might involve some voluntary transfer of populations. A clean frontier and non-interference in each other's internal affairs, social or national, must be the basis for future friendship and co-operation. Failing these, the experience of the last 200 years has shown that for Poland Russian-German friendship means enslavement and Russian-German war means ruin and devastation; while for Russia every spell of friendship with Germany meant giving the Germans opportunities for building up overwhelming strength with which to resume their traditional 'expansion against the East.'

(3) THE CURZON LINE

The thirteenth of President Wilson's Points postulated 'an independent Polish State . . . which should include the territories inhabited by indisputably Polish populations'; and by Article 87 of the Treaty of Versailles Poland agreed that her boundaries not laid down in that Treaty shall 'be subsequently determined by the Principal Allied and Associated Powers.' These frontiers were the subject of careful study and of discussion in which the Bolish case was fully stated and considered, whereas Russia was without official representation or direct influence. The only counterweight to the very active pressure exerted by the Poles was the thought about a more distant future, when Russia would have recovered; this was present especially in the minds of the British delegation.

On 21st April 1919, the Commission on Polish Affairs reported on the northern sector of Poland's eastern frontier, down to about Kholm, agreement on that province being delayed by British doubts concerning its eastern, predominantly Ukrainian districts. Eventually, however, the whole province was assigned to Poland, with the River Bug for frontier. The northern sector of the frontier was then approved on 8th December 1919, in a declaration of the Supreme Council, signed by Clemenceau as president. The southern sector was fixed in the East-Galician Statute, adopted on 20th November 1919, but cancelled a month later in deference to Polish opposition, which turned the French; still, the Allied views on what was indisputably Polish territory in Galicia were re-stated in the 'Certain Frontiers' Treaty of 10th August 1920.

In July 1920, after the defeat of the Polish expedition

against Kiev, the Bolsheviks gained a temporary ascendancy and the Poles had to seek Allied protection: a
chance now seemed to open of establishing the frontier
previously sanctioned by the Supreme Council. With
Polish consent it was proposed to Soviet Russia by Lord
Curzon (and thus became associated with his name) as
an armistice line to which the Polish forces were to
retire pending a peace conference to be held in London.
But this was not a mere demarcation line suggested by
momentary considerations: the intention was that the
'provisional' should endure.

Still, all approach on the part of the Allies was viewed
with supreme suspicion by the Bolsheviks, who failed
to appreciate the wish of the more far-sighted among
the Allies for an ethnically just frontier between Poland
and Russia. At that time the Bolsheviks seemed likely to
overrun the whole of Poland, and their concern was not
with frontiers; M. Chicherin, in his reply of 18th July
1920, desires 'guarantees that Poland will cease to be an
instrument of aggression and intrigues against the
workers and peasants of Soviet Russia. . . .' The note was
propaganda addressed to the Poles over the heads of the
Allies, rather than an instrument for negotiation. Appeal-
ing to Polish nationalism, Soviet Russia offered, in her
own peace conditions, to meet 'the interests and wishes
of the Polish people,' provided they drew closer to the
Soviets 'in their internal life,' and Chicherin criticized
the Curzon Line as 'elaborated by the Supreme Council
in some parts under the pressure of counter-revolutionary
Russian elements'; but when offering an example of its
unfairness to the Poles he named 'the region of Kholm'
though the Curzon Line assigns all that region to the
Poles. It is not clear whether Chicherin's citation was
ignorance or mockery. But those who quote his note

usually refrain from mentioning either its basic provisos or its illuminating example.

The Bolsheviks failed to reach Warsaw; soon the tide turned, and the Poles regained complete superiority. They rejected pleas for self-determination for Lithuania, White Russia, and the Ukraine, and a proposal for a plebiscite in East Galicia. At Riga they dictated their own terms to the Bolsheviks. The Bolsheviks, in acute danger from Wrangel, could not refuse Polish demands; they may even have calculated, in the revolutionary mood of the period, that the more White Russian and Ukrainian territory was placed under the Poles, the greater the chance of a successful social and national revolt.

Although great care was taken to include within the Curzon Line all territories with a Polish population which could be assigned to Poland without adding much larger numbers of non-Poles, the line was a minimum frontier for Poland, and did not preclude improvements should the Poles establish valid ethnic claims beyond it. What number of Poles were there east of the Curzon Line at the census of 1931?

It is not possible to give a fully satisfactory answer. The Poles extended the province of Lvov far west of the Curzon Line, including in it West-Galician territory with about 800,000 Poles and hardly any Ukrainians, thus obliterating the ethnic border between East and West Galicia. Further, of the Ukrainians in East Galicia 60 per cent were entered as speaking 'Ukrainian,' while 40 per cent, inhabiting the same districts and differing in no way from the others in their speech, were registered as speaking the 'Ruski' language (which does not mean Russian, for which there is a different name in Polish, 'Rosyjski,' and a separate column in the statistical tables). Or again, in the province of Polesie, where there were very few Poles, two-thirds of the population, 707,000 in number, were registered as speaking the 'local' (tutejszy) language, which was no other than White Russian.

Such sources of confusion can be easily traced. But it is impossible to check with any degree of accuracy misleading entries in the census itself. In certain cases religion supplies a corrective to nationality figures; a Greek Orthodox Russian peasant will be much more amenable to his language being misstated in the statistical returns than to any tampering with his religion. Less reliable is the same criterion in the case of the Greek Catholics. With them 'occasional conformity' was by no means rare, and may account for statistical deviations. Worst of all is the case of the Roman Catholic White Russians, one of the most primitive peoples in Europe: Roman Catholicism was known in Western Russia as the 'Polish faith,' and White Russians would in that sense let themselves be described as 'Poles.'

At the census of 1931 there were in East Galicia nearly 1,600,000 Roman Catholics, over 3,000,000 Greek Catholics, and about 550,000 Jews. It is, to say the least, remarkable that between 1911 and 1931 the Roman Catholics in East Galicia should have increased by more than a third, while the number of Greek Catholics seems to have suffered a slight decline. Roman Catholics and Greek Catholics live intermixed in the same districts and even in the same communes, were affected more or less in the same way by war or emigration, while the natural increase was, if anything, greater among the Greek Catholics. There was, no doubt, an influx of Polish officials and of a certain number of officially assisted settlers to East Galicia between 1919 and 1939. Still, the growth in the number of Roman Catholics and the absence of increase in that of the Greek Catholics can only be explained by wrong entries or 'conversions' of a political and social character—it was often advantageous to Greek Catholics seeking employment with the State, or at Polish manor houses, to declare themselves Roman Catholics. If the total of genuine and autochthonous Poles in East Galicia is placed at 1,250,000, the figure will hardly prove an underestimate.

The population of the northern provinces east of the Curzon Line (Vilna, Novogrodek, Polesie, Volhynia, and the easternmost part of Bialystok) comprised in 1931 almost 1,800,000 Roman Catholics, 3,500,000 Greek Orthodox, and about 550,000 Jews. The Greek Orthodox were either Ukrainians or White Russians. Of the Roman Catholics probably almost 200,000 were Lithuanians, Germans, Czechs, etc.; and if those who have to be booked as White Russians are placed somewhere half-way between the Russian overestimate of 1897 and the Polish underestimate of 1931, we obtain for them the figure of 500,000–600,000. Lastly, here, too, in certain districts a remarkable increase can be noticed in the numbers of Roman Catholics, probably due to an importation of officials and settlers. The number of genuine, autochthonous Poles in these northern provinces will not have been very much more than 1,000,000. Thus, on a liberal estimate, there were hardly more than 2,250,000 to 2,500,000 Poles east of the Curzon Line, in a total population of over 11,000,000.

(4) RUSSIA'S WAY WITH INVADERS

In 1941–3 the year 1812 was in everybody's mind. We asked: where the Man broke, will the ghastly Machine be shattered? By 1810 the luminous drama of

the French Revolution and Napoleon was losing its
inner lustre, the splendid orb was getting dim in a weary
afternoon, values and ideas were waning in the magni-
tude of the Imperial structure and the vastness of the
Emperor's plans and undertakings. And yet these heirs
to high endeavour, though in moral decline, how distant
are they from the 'ice-cold lust' of frenzied, organized
hatreds translated into conquests bare of message! The
figure of the Emperor stands out, even against the flames
of Moscow, even at the Beresina bridges.

> . . . cette ombre altière et péremptoire
> Que tu feras toujours sur le mur de l'histoire!

Napoleon's greatness heightens the feeling of disaster
when he loses command and, with jointed limbs, staggers
through the puppet-show. 'I was carried away by events,'
he said in December 1812; and, self-centred and callous,
he next remarked on the one step from the sublime to
the ridiculous. The indraft of Russia had seized him and
he had meandered into an abyss. The elements were
against him—so they had been against the Spanish Ar-
mada; and in both cases it was found convenient to stress
their workings. But when Napoleon, from the Kremlin
window, gazed at the blazing city, he spoke of men:
'They themselves are setting it afire. What a people!
They are Scythians!' 'Well-ordered capitals' had
received him with convenient submission—these were
'excesses unworthy of . . . a great nation.' 'To burn one's
own cities! . . . A demon inspires these men! What
savage determination! What a people! What a people!'
And shortly before his death he said about Borodino:
'The most terrible of all my battles was that before
Moscow. The French showed themselves worthy of victory, and the Russians of being invincible.' M. Tarlé is

right: 'Not the cold and not Russia's vast expanses conquered Napoleon, but the resistance of the Russian
people.'

Napoleon's Invasion of Russia, 1812,[1] by one of the
most eminent of the pre-Revolution historians, first appeared in Russian in 1938, and its pragmatic outlook
is significant, for it clearly envisages an impending German attack, and turns to the past for guidance and
assurance. Though the book will not fully satisfy the
student of military or diplomatic history, it supplies the
general reader with a well written and well informed
account of the war, and important original contributions clearly appear in the chapters on 'The Russian
People and the Invasion' and on 'Partisan Warfare.'
Next there are the perennial problems of 1812, always
open to reinterpretation or to new analysis: the interplay
in the Russian retreat of plan and of action imposed by
circumstances; the burning of Moscow (how far was it
deliberate?); and, lastly, Kutuzov's policy after Moscow
—for it was policy rather than strategy.

On 18th May 1812, General Count Narbonne saw the
Tsar at Vilna. 'Emperor Alexander,' he reports, 'seems
prepared to lose two or three battles, but feigns determination to go on fighting in Tartary if need be.' 'This,'
writes M. Tarlé, 'is the earliest mention of the formula
that, with certain purely stylistic variations, Alexander
kept repeating throughout the war of 1812.'

'On my side are space and time,' he said—did this
imply an idea of luring Napoleon to his doom in the
vast expanse of Russia? Even this conception appears
full-fledged at an early date—as conceptions usually do.
(Moreover there was the precedent of Charles XII and

---

[1] *Napoleon's Invasion of Russia, 1812*. By Eugene Tarlé. Allen and
Unwin. 1942.

Poltava.) General Marian Kukiel, in his great work on *The War of 1812*, traces the idea of a defensive retreat (and also of 'scorched earth') in two memoranda drawn up in 1809 and 1810 by Wolzogen, a Württemberger in Russian service; in plans developed by Barclay de Tolly after Friedland and in 1810; in a memorandum written by Gneisenau in May–June 1812; and even in a letter addressed to the Tsar, on the outbreak of war, by Count Rostopchin, who could hardly have voiced it had it not been talk *à la mode*.

Still, it is quite possible to envisage an idea, play with it, profess it, even flaunt it, without truly embracing it; and naturally a plan which implied the abandoning of wide stretches of Russian land was more readily accepted by foreigners serving Russia than by Russians. Yet circumstances, common sense, and a wholesome fear of Napoleon's genius imposed on the Russian commanders —on Kutuzov no less than on the 'foreigner' Barclay de Tolly—the strategy which alone could achieve victory; but while applying it these commanders were subjected to the bitterest criticisms and attacks. Here then was a correct idea which sharply ran counter to national and professional instincts, but which finally was enforced by the logic of events and the pressure of circumstances.

Two knowledgeable witnesses, Liprandi, Head Quartermaster of the Sixth Corps, and Count von Toll, Quartermaster-General of the First Army (Barclay's), are quoted by M. Tarlé on the question whether it was long-term policy or day-to-day expediency which guided the Russian commanders. Liprandi writes:

> I venture to conclude that neither before Smolensk nor until Moscow itself did we have any defined plan of action. Everything happened according to circumstance. When the foe was distant, our leaders showed determina-

tion to give general battle, and according to all calculations they thought they would win. Once the foe approached, everything changed. The retreat was resumed, and this, too, was justified by accurate calculations. The whole immense correspondence of Barclay and of Kutuzov himself clearly proves that they themselves did not know what they would or should do.

And von Toll maintains in his memoirs that

at the beginning of the war, positively no one on the Russian staff at Vilna had the least idea of the part which the colossal expanses of Russia would play. This was realized only as the war progressed. The retreat had been dictated by Barclay's reluctance to risk the destruction of the army in the first days of the war.

Barclay maintained an 'army in being,' and wisely avoided decisive engagements while Napoleon's forces were double his own; by the time Borodino was reached there was an approximate equality of numbers: and on moral grounds it was unthinkable to abandon Moscow without resistance.

Napoleon from the very outset sought a decisive engagement and an early peace. But the Russian armies eluded him; before Vitebsk he was so eager for a general engagement that 'he ordered Murat and Viceroy Eugène not to hinder separate detachments of the Russian Army from uniting with the main Russian forces.' But when about to give battle, he found once more an empty camp and a deserted city. Here, on July 28th, he held a conference.

If the Russian army was retreating from weakness, that was one thing; but what if this were a deliberate strategic plan? 'Never do what your enemy wants you to do' . . . that was one of Napoleon's strictest rules. The Emperor concluded the conference with the solemn announcement that he meant to end the campaign in Vitebsk.

For only two days he abode by this decision. Next, he would end the campaign at Smolensk. Count Daru, Secretary of State and Intendant-General of the Grand Army, protested: 'If we are short of provisions here in Vitebsk, what will happen later?' And, again: 'Not only our troops, Sire, but we ourselves fail to understand either the aims or the necessity of this war.' As Napoleon approached Smolensk, he thought he held the Russians in his hands; but they slipped away once more. Even Murat now begged him to stop. Napoleon assented: 'The first Russian campaign is concluded.' But on the night of August 24th to 25th he set out from Smolensk.

Kutuzov, who now replaced Barclay, was a real Russian, with an instinctive understanding of Russian needs and potentialities. Expansive and yet secretive, naïve and sly, he was accommodating on the surface but stubborn deep down. To everybody's surprise, on his second day at headquarters he ordered a retreat, thus reproducing the strategy decried as treason in his predecessor. Later on he accepted battle at Borodino, because, in the words of Clausewitz, 'the voice of the Court, of the Army, of all Russia, forced his hand.' The Russians lost half their army, but were not defeated. Was another battle to be fought this side of Moscow, or was the city to be abandoned? Kutuzov, having listened in Council to those who advised resistance, abruptly closed it with the words: 'By the authority granted me by the Tsar and the Fatherland, I command retirement.' On September 14th, from Poklannaya Hill, Napoleon beheld Moscow, the great Eurasian capital, 'the key to world domination.' He was congratulated: 'Here, at last, is the famous city!' He replied: 'It was time.' Now he waited for a deputation from Moscow. It never came. When he entered the city he found a vast emptiness. 'What a terrible desert!' he exclaimed. And one of his soldiers writes: 'I passed through immense squares and broad streets. I glanced into the windows of every house and, not finding a soul within, I grew numb with horror.'

At this point Count Rostopchin, Governor and Commander-in-Chief of Moscow, crosses the stage—a weird figure, a Frenchified Russian aristocrat, lacking the culture of either nation, a bully and a coward, cruel and absurd, *un faux bonhomme*, deceitful and credulous, an arch-reactionary who at one juncture tried to play the popular showman and demagogue; a jester with a streak of old Karamazov in him. And yet it seems by now pretty well established that it was he who played the decisive part in the burning of Moscow. Later on he sometimes denied it, and on other occasions boasted of it. But on August 24th he wrote to Bagration that if the Russians had to evacuate Moscow 'they will burn the city to ashes, and Napoleon, instead of booty, will get only the spot where the capital had been.'

Here is [writes M. Tarlé] Police Superintendent Voronenko's official report to the Moscow Administration: 'On 14 September, at five in the morning, Count Rostopchin ordered me to go to the Wine Arcade and the Custom House . . . and in the event of a sudden entry by enemy troops, to destroy everything with fire, which order I carried out in various places as far as it was possible in sight of the enemy until ten o'clock in the evening. . . .'

It is more than probable that independently of Rostopchin's arrangements other persons left behind in Moscow risked their lives to destroy anything that might be useful to the enemy. Finally, many fires were doubtless started by the French, while looting.

Henceforth 'the will to destroy the intruders became national in the full sense of the word. Napoleon had gambled on terrorizing Russia, and lost.'

On October 19th Napoleon left Moscow. And now starts a game on the part of Kutuzov, incomprehensible to his contemporaries, and puzzling to historians. 'Kutuzov . . . had his own firm plan,' writes M. Tarlé, 'and . . . ceased paying attention to anything but his plan.' From the moment of Napoleon's departure from Moscow he did not doubt that the French would leave Russia and without any battles—'consequently he thought battle unnecessary.' He 'did not want to catch up with Napoleon, and nothing could change his mind.' He admitted that he was building 'golden bridges' for the enemy, and limited himself to a 'parallel pursuit,' avoiding encounters. He had his 'political speculations' —of a supreme isolationist. Russia's interest was served by the French evacuating her territory, and he did not care about Europe. His closest collaborators believed that at the Beresina Kutuzov allowed Napoleon to escape. 'Beresina! Fateful name, fateful river where the misfortunes of mankind could have ended, but did not end, continuing for three more years!' exclaims a German writer. But is it so certain that Kutuzov was in a position to attack? He knew the state of his own army, which during the pursuit from Moscow to Vilna had shrunk to less than a third of its size. And why take risks in battle against Napoleon when the Russian earth and its seasons, and its people prowling round the fast crumbling host, were anyhow annihilating it without respite or mercy?

After 1812 it was, according to Kutuzov,

hard and dangerous to undertake a new war against Napoleon, and it was entirely unnecessary. The Russian people had asserted their rights, vanquished the invincible enemy, and won immortal glory. Why liberate and strengthen the Germans, who as Russia's neighbours were potential enemies? Why shed Russian blood for the Germans, who would one day perhaps shed the blood of the grandsons and great-grandsons of the very Russian soldiers who were now to be driven to fight Napoleon for the liberation of Germany?

In the end Kutuzov's policy cost Russia further heavy sacrifices—and who was right, he or Alexander, backed, for once, by Russian public opinion? Could Russia have been truly safe had Napoleon's Empire survived? M. Tarlé wrote his book during Russia's pre-1941 isolation and isolationism, and this undoubtedly colours its outlook.

Before 1812, French dominion used to improve the condition of the labour classes in conquered countries. But there is no sign of Napoleon having seriously thought of emancipating the peasant-serfs of Russia. In the first provinces he entered, in Lithuania and White Russia, the big landowners were Poles whom he tried to win over to his side; and there alone, where no ties of nationality bound the peasants to the gentry, did revolts break out—they were put down with French help. In Great Russia, where 'during the entire existence of serfdom, scarcely a year passed without some peasant disturbance,' popular discontents were sunk 'in the immense surge of anger' against the invader. 'The threat that hung over Russia, the enslavement of the entire Russian nation by the alien conqueror, became the first consideration.' Numerous examples of spontaneous action by the peasants are quoted by M. Tarlé, and of their share in partisan warfare which was to prove a deadly scourge for the French. But the Government and the big landowners looked on such peasant activities with misgivings, and obstructed them. 'What will they do after the war if we now train and arm them?' is the question which invariably troubles uneasy consciences with regard to unwanted allies. In fact, the Russian peasants 'thought that by their heroic struggle against Napoleon they had "earned their freedom" and that they would receive it from the Tsar.' But in Alexander's manifesto of 1814, only one line referred to them: 'The peasants, our loyal people, will be recompensed by God.'

(5) THE RUSSIAN PEASANT

Sir John Maynard's book[1] on the history of the Russian village in the last eighty years is written with a thorough knowledge of village life and peasant masses, acquired, in the first place, by service in India, where as an administrator he had to face similar problems on an equally gigantic scale.

The U.S.S.R. covers well-nigh a continent, and the Soviet Government controls the economic life of nearly 200,000,000 people. Of these, two-thirds still live in villages, forming some 26,000,000 peasant households: potentially the greatest force in the Soviet Union. No system can work, and no government can survive, which has the peasantry, and its formidable negative strength, against it. Have the Bolsheviks found in the collective farm the solution of their greatest problem? Can it harmonize their own principles and conceptions with the deepest instincts of the peasant, and reconcile the requirements of modern agricultural production and of a modern national economy with his desires and wants?

[1] *The Russian Peasant and other Studies.* By Sir John Maynard. Gollancz. 1942.

For 'peasant agriculture is not merely a means of liveli-hood: it is a way of life.' One needs to have lived in an East-European village to appreciate the full meaning of these words, and to understand the power of the peasant community; governments and masters pass away, but the village commune goes on, a close, self-conscious congregation.

Yet even in dealing with the land problem 'all Russian régimes have been sudden and arbitrary,' have chopped and changed, and shown little regard for property or prescriptive rights. Experiments (and blunders) on a vertiginous scale did not start with the Bolsheviks, who merely quickened the pace and sharpened the edge of planning and interference. The economic results of the first great modern agrarian reform, the Statutes of 1861 abolishing serfdom, were disappointing: more than half of the land in Russia was assigned to the peasants, still their holdings were mostly insufficient in size (about 30 per cent were downright uneconomic), short of pasture and woods, and burdened with redemption dues. In about three-fourths of European Russia, their tenure was communal: the *mir* (village meeting) had control over the choice of crops and over cultivation, and in most of Great Russia had power to redistribute the land periodically, which was generally done 'in accordance with the labouring capacity of each unit.' By 1905 the peasants had greatly increased the total area of their holdings by purchases from the gentry, but the pressure of the population had grown even more: the land was a burning problem in the Revolution of 1905. The First Duma planned to expropriate the squires at a fair price; this might have temporarily satisfied the peasants, but would have lowered the output of Russian agriculture: the cultivation of peasant holdings, consisting of scat-

tered strips, was poor whatever the system of tenure.
After the Duma had been forcibly dissolved, the Prime
Minister, Stolypin, launched a scheme for establishing
compact, economically sufficient peasant farms, free of
communal control, with their ownership vested in individuals, and not as hitherto in families. 'The audacity
and vastness of the design are typical of Russia, whether
it be Russia of the Tsars or Russia of the Bolsheviks.'
The area concerned 'amounted to 320,000,000 acres and
12,000,000 households.' Everything was done to facilitate the changeover from communal to individual land
tenure, and to favour 'the separators' or 'seceders.'
Three stages were envisaged in the procedure: (1) establishing separate property in the strips of arable; (2) con-
solidating them into blocks; (3) removal of the farmhouse
from the clustered village to the holding. By 1916 about
one-fifth of the peasant holdings had been 'individua-
lized,' but only a small percentage of their owners had
chosen to remove from the villages. Agriculture gained
through the change, and so did the hard-headed and
hard-fisted, the most intelligent and enterprising, among
the peasants. 'The "strong and sober" . . .' writes Sir
John Maynard, 'upon whom Stolypin proposed to build,
appeared to be benefiting, as the strong and sober—
fortified by the science of arithmetic—usually do, in
their dealings with those who are neither strong nor
sober, or not arithmetically minded.'

The working of the Stolypin scheme had to be sus-
pended in 1916: peasant soldiers were growing restless
about changes carried through in the villages in their
absence (this is also one reason why the Revolution of
1917 disintegrated the Russian Army—the peasant soldiers set off for home to mind their own interests in the
village). The 'separators' were never popular with the

others, and the Provisional Government in 1917 repealed the Stolypin Acts, while in many villages the *mir*, whose power increased with the decline of central authority, forced 'seceders' back into the community. The big estates were seized, transferring the last 20 per cent of land to the peasant. This the peasants wished to add either to the communal holdings or to their individual farms: none thought of new experiments. In those early years 'the Communist Government, most accomplished of experimentalists and opportunists,' passed laws of merely theoretical interest. The Civil War was raging, the Soviets were fighting for their life, and the fear lest a counter-revolution would restore the estates to the big landowners secured peasant support for them. This was not the time for enforcing new experiments. Next to survival, the securing of food for the towns and the army was the chief concern of the Bolsheviks. Peasants produce for sale to pay taxes, debts, rent, or to buy industrial produce—now payments could hardly be collected, while the towns had very little to offer. Moreover war, foreign and civil, had depleted the livestock in the villages, agricultural implements and machinery had greatly deteriorated, production had shrunk to an alarming degree; the climax came when the drought of 1920–1 in the fertile Black Earth zone, from the Volga to the Western Ukraine, produced a terrible catastrophe—several million people died of hunger, and agriculture suffered still further through the enormous losses which occurred in horses, cattle, etc.

The New Economic Policy—the well-known N.E.P. —was a strategic retreat of Communism, and a reversion to the Stolypin economy. The 'strong and the sober,' if they prevailed in their village, had to be left free to remodel its life. 'In almost every village there was a struggle between those who desired to maintain the *mir*, and those who wished to leave it or break it up.' In 1922–4, over 8,000,000 acres were resettled in individual holdings. Peasant capitalism was in the ascendant—and there is no harder taskmaster and more cruel usurer than the rich peasant (the word *kulak*, meaning 'a fist,' had for generations denoted a peasant usurer). The peasant who had oxen, horses, implements, and seed enslaved those who needed them to work their scanty holdings, and exacted exorbitant tribute either in a share of the produce, or in labour services, or in both. By 1928, the rich peasants formed about 4 per cent of the village population, the peasant proletariat about 30 per cent, the rest consisting of middling peasants.

The turn away from N.E.P. started with industry and trade in 1924—plan and not price was to guide economic action, but for a time State industry was combined with a free agriculture. It was not till December 1928 that the fifteenth Congress of the Communist Party decided to restrict the leasing of land and hiring of labour, and declared in favour of a gradual collectivization of agriculture, but by example rather than by compulsion. 'No doubt,' writes Sir John Maynard, 'there were reasons of social policy for undertaking the great transformation with all the risks and difficulties which were involved. . . . But far more convincing and urgent were the administrative and economic arguments.' For certain types of agriculture, big farms are essential, and such farms can best be fitted into a planned economy. But it would have been vain to wait for voluntary change.

There was prolonged hesitation before the final blow was struck. When it came, it was stunning in its impact. In January 1930, the aims of complete collectivization within three years, and the 'liquidation' of the *kulaks*,

were announced. The latter meant that persons number-
ing, with their families, some five millions, were to be
dispossessed of their properties, and in many cases driven
from their homes.

Stalin's conversion of small-scale into large-scale agriculture 'was a greater and more arduous achievement
than the overthrow of the Tsar and the November
insurrection.' The unpopularity of the rich peasants in
the villages, and a tradition of village Communism,
facilitated the overthrow of the *kulaks*. But 'it is a
horrifying picture. . . . Yesterday encouraged to increase
and multiply the subsistence of the family; to-day ousted
from home and property, and exiled to a precarious
livelihood.' Together with usurers and oppressors
perished intelligent, enterprising workers: it was one of
those gigantic, fantastic transformations which can be
conceived and carried out in Russia. It was rendered possible by the now abundant Soviet production of modern
agricultural machinery and of manufactured goods: the
State, which imposed new forms of life and work on the
village, had something substantial to offer. At the beginning of 1933, 14,500,000 peasant households had been
'collectivized,' by July 1936, 90 per cent of the total.
Individual property was allowed to continue in the house,
garden allotment, in poultry, in one or two cows, etc.
But the wide fields outside the villages, covering in the
average *kolkhoz* several thousand acres, were henceforth
tilled collectively with modern machinery and by modern
methods. Especially the younger folk in the village took
to the new system: it is a 'machine-minded' generation,
and the lad who has driven a tractor, a steam-plough,
or a harvester, will not easily resign himself to the
old primitive, slow, and laborious methods; moreover,
in the collective he enjoys full membership and is

freed from the domestic tyranny of the peasant household.

Undoubtedly, even if carried through with the greatest consideration, such changes would be fraught with dangers. In Soviet Russia excessive zeal and ruthlessness in certain officials, sometimes joined to insufficient technical knowledge, brought about, especially in distant regions, tragedies and losses on quite a serious scale. Yet taken as a whole the change seems to have been justified and successful: it has produced a new type of agriculture with far greater prospects for the future than small-holdings offer, especially in the production of cereals. In the past, peasant agriculture was mostly inferior to that of the big capitalist estates: the *kolkhoz* is an attempt at reviving large-scale agricultural production under a Socialist system. Moreover it has created a new type of peasant: 'a factory hand working in the open air.' For him 'collectivization is a step up on the social ladder.'

7.

ANTI-SEMITISM

EIGHTEEN AUTHORS, Gentiles and Jews, have contributed to this work,[1] all of them men and women of academic standing, professors at Harvard, Yale, and various younger universities, from New York to California. Carefully planned and blended, the book is serious in tone and purpose, and frank and courageous in substance—there is an aim, but no propaganda. The essays contributed by Gentiles are, on the whole, more remarkable than those by Jews, perhaps owing to an inherent natural selection: it requires more personality in a Gentile to take a dispassionate or a truly Christian interest in the Jewish question than for a Jew to be disturbed about it. Moreover, most of the Jewish contributors seem to be non-national Jews, some with an uneasy duality in their souls. There is no essay on Zionism, and when it enters incidentally, Gentiles show more understanding for it than the half-assimilated Jews. The 'Gentile World' of this book, for practical purposes, is the United States—an important segment, harbouring almost one-half of the Jewish race; still, only a segment. Even within that limited framework there is a serious omission; while sample descriptions are given of Jewry in 'a medium-sized, metropolitan centre of the American industrial Mid-West,' and in Stamford, Con-

[1] *Jews in a Gentile World: the Problem of Anti-Semitism.* Edited by Isacque Graeber and Steuart Henderson Britt. The Macmillan Company, New York. 1942.

necticut, there is no monograph on New York City, the greatest Jewish community ever known, which now comprises about one-fifth of world-Jewry and about two-fifths of that of America.

The attitude of the Gentile contributors is one of deep concern at the ever-widening stream of anti-Semitic prejudice and hatred. In an introductory essay on 'Anti-Semitism: Challenge to Christian Culture,' Professor C. J. Friedrich indicts it as 'the most blatant outward manifestation of the decadence of Western culture, 'an amoral pattern of behaviour' which has emerged because previously cherished ethical norms are 'wearing thin.' 'The anti-Christian nature of the Nazi reaction furnishes the explanation for the fact that anti-Semitism is the core and centre of the "revolutionary ideal" of the Nazis.' 'The ferocity of this war . . . cannot be adequately explained in terms of the clash of material interests. It is a struggle round the spiritual destiny of the planet.' And in the closing paragraphs of the book Professor Raymond Kennedy writes: 'The Jewish problem . . . is vitally linked with the broader issue now being fought'; the Nazis 'seem to see this clearly, for they habitually make reference to the Jewish question in their diatribes against democracy. . . . It is almost as though they realized that anti-Semitism, even in relatively mild form, is one of the weak points in our democracy.' It may 'eventually strike at the very heart of a democratic culture'; but if this culture is 'worth striving for, here is a test of the true strength of our national democratic ideals.'

Anti-Semitism shoots up and spreads in times of un-settlement and confusion: 'a manifestation of social disorganization.' Its sociological and psychological aspects are examined by Professors J. O. Hertzler and

Talcott Parsons, J. F. Brown and Ellis Freeman; and their essays dovetail so closely that they can best be treated jointly and quoted indiscriminately. Throughout history the Jew has been the scapegoat in times of crisis; and there is a peculiar technique of scapegoatry. Social dislocation—for instance after a defeat or an economic collapse—produces feelings of insecurity and frustration, usually coloured by a sense of injustice; and these tend to engender a vague and diffuse hostility and intensely bitter resentments—a 'free-floating' aggression. The authors of disaster or frustration may be 'too powerful and awesome,' or may be beyond the reach of the sufferers; or there may be reluctance to fix the guilt in the right quarter. Hatreds within one's own community are usually frowned upon, but not hatreds against non-members, which, by diverting latent hostilities and canalizing discontents, tend to consolidate the internal coherence of the community or nation. A 'conspicuous but helpless and defenceless minority' is 'a cheap and safe enemy,' and anti-Semitism 'a socially acceptable way of expending repressed and pent-up aggressive energy.'

'In times of national stress and insecurity, what better scapegoat could be found than the "stranger in our midst"?' Violent emotions seek 'face-to-face objects,' and the ubiquitous, mysterious Jew offers a perfect target. To be well known, yet unknown; neither completely strange, nor truly a member of the community; to be a '"foreign" element which is at the same time close enough to have constant relations with the "native" element'—means to be 'subject to all sorts of suspicions and accusations.' That the Jew is 'the biological and cultural equal of the Gentile' avails him nothing—'we love, hate, and fear our cultural equals more than our

cultural inferiors.' Moreover, there is more relish in
degrading and humiliating one's equal or superior than
in stressing an obvious inferiority; and there is the kind
of 'patriotism' which offers to the depressed and frustrated an easy avenue to restoring their self-esteem at
the expense of others, chiefly of the Jew. 'The pattern
of sentiments seems to be somewhat as follows: "I may
not be a successful person . . . but there is one thing you
can't deny—I am just as much an American (or German
or Englishman) as anybody." . . . National identification
allows the individual to participate in the glory of the
achievements of *his* nation and relieves him of the blame
for lack of *personal* achievements.' As a mass-movement
which enjoys general social approbation, anti-Semitism
becomes a 'heart-warming experience'; and in a
genuinely anti-Semitic environment it 'has for each
individual so obscure an origin in his biography that he
is prone to account for it as something congenital.'
Indeed, 'anti-Semitism . . . assumes the impressiveness
of a law of nature.'

The situation is aggravated by the Jew being 'a
widely dispersed, alien minority'—were he 'merely a
local problem in a single country he would not have
attracted much attention. But because he is a continuous
minority in all the communicating lands of the Western
world, the apprehensions regarding him as a minority
were transferable, interchangeable, and even cumulative
to a degree.' A common Gentile attitude and tradition
has grown up with regard to the Jews, and has been com-
municated and continued.

A stereotype has arisen of the Jew 'with exaggerated
racial physiognomic characteristics, with . . . a double
set of ethical and moral values for his own race and for
outsiders, with predatory business habits—a parsi-

ANTI-SEMITISM 117

monious and unpleasantly aggressive individual.' Undoubtedly some Jews possess all these characteristics,
and a number show some: or such a stereotype could not
arise—it does not invent non-existent traits, but exag-
gerates, distorts, and over-generalizes them, while omit-
ting favourable characteristics 'which are as "typical"
of the racial "character" as are any of the unfavourable
traits.'

'Group stereotypes are strongly developed in caste
situations,' writes Professor Kennedy, and the Jews are
'a religio-national group, occupying the status of a
quasi-caste in American society.' Heredity of status is
more pronounced in their case than in that of other
white minority groups; social intercourse and intermarriage with them are restricted in a manner qualita-
tively differing from that ordinarily produced by
national dislikes or religious contrasts; and 'qualities
and accomplishments which are valued as virtues' in
Gentiles, 'are considered vices' in Jews—'a very common mark of caste.' The self-made man is a hero of
American national folk-lore, says Dr. Kennedy, 'but
only so far as caste lines allow. The success of the Jews
in business or the professions is not generally praised;
rather is it regarded as a threat. They are not said to
have made a success of the clothing business and the
cinema industry; they have "got control" of them. . . .
This kind of attack reaches a climax in sinister fabrica-
tions concerning the machinations of "the international
Jewish bankers."' That Jewish control over American
economic life 'is clearly a myth can readily be proven,'
writes Dr. Parsons; and Miss Miriam Beard contributes
an essay on 'Anti-Semitism—Product of Economic
Myths.' But common sense, proofs, or arguments are
inoperative against myths surcharged with emotion; and

still more against delusionary figments bordering on mental pathology. These emerge in times of extreme stress, and accuse the Jews of 'ritual murder,' of causing the Black Death (in the fourteenth century) or the two World Wars (in the twentieth), of plotting for 'world dominion,' etc. (the thesis of the 'Protocols of the Elders of Zion' continued to find credence even after they were conclusively exposed as a forgery).

Much can be said, and some things are said in this book, about Jewish peculiarities which evoke anti-Semitism, and about the deleterious effect which anti-Semitism has in turn on the Jews—discrimination, humiliations, and persecutions do not as a rule bring out the most lovable traits in human beings, or increase their sanity, or make them into pleasant companions. But even those among the contributors who touch upon these matters seem to feel that it is useless to approach the problem of the Jews and anti-Semitism from the angle of real, or alleged, Jewish peculiarities. There is something infinitely greater and more fundamental behind this terrifying problem of world history: and it is terrifying for the anti-Semites almost as much as it is for their victims.

What is it that has aroused those passions and phobias in so many lands, through so many centuries? Understand and explain the problem as much as you may, there remains a hard, insoluble core, incomprehensible and inexplicable. And so one is driven back to the most obvious answer: anti-Semitism is the world reaction to a most unique social and historical phenomenon, the wanderings of the Jews and their survival as a people.

The Jews originated and developed at the crossroads of early civilization, and were 'subject from the earliest days to the push and pull of powerful and advanced

neighbours'—Egyptians, Assyrians, Babylonians, etc.—
even then 'they lacked a secure land basis.' Professor
Stonequist continues: 'The prominence which the Jews
have given to the Exodus from Egypt, to the period of
wandering in the desert under the leadership of Moses,
and to the search for the Promised Land may be taken
as indicative of the importance of their spatial instabi-
lity. . . .' The Jewish movements into Europe were 'part
of a population shift of Mediterranean peoples,' says
Professor Carleton Stevens Coon. What differentiated
the Jews was 'not their initial racial make-up, but the
fact that they were destined to retain their religious and
ethnic solidarity indefinitely.' One Gentile contributor
after another dwells on this fact. The Jews, a people
without a country, continue to exist as a nation. 'Whether
or not the Jews are a race . . . they must be designated
as a nationality.' Normally a culture is the product of its
land, attached to it and identified with it. 'But the
Jewish culture is always a foreign culture—an undigested
element.' The Jews 'remain, in spite of themselves, a
culture-within-a-culture, no matter where they are';
and as 'all cultures strain after consistency,' the presence
of this strange element produces irritation and appears
to the majority culture 'like a parasitical growth inter-
fering with its own normal functioning.' The Jew
assumes 'a half-way position relative to the Gentile's
world, neither completely in nor completely out.' And
as Dr. Kennedy bluntly puts it, 'a Jew either regards
himself . . . or is regarded by others (even though he may
not like it) as primarily a Jew, whatever his other
nationality membership.'

'The "Jewish problem,"' writes Professor Carl
Mayer, 'is . . . in the order of a "mystery"'; it is ultimately inexplicable, 'incapable of theoretical solution,'

and 'impervious to rational analysis; the Jewish people
represent a sociologically *unique* phenomenon and defy
all attempts at general definition.' They became 'a
people by the act of the Sinaitic revelation.' 'If they are
a church, then they are a church *plus* a people or, rather,
a church of flesh and blood.' Re-created in the Dispersion
'as a people in the "spirit" . . . they seem to be charac-
terized by a strange and peculiar kind of unreality. . . .
They seem to have . . . an existence without existence,
lacking all "substance" . . . they seem to have no history
at all.' 'The impression has always prevailed that there
is something strange, uncanny, and therefore incomprehensible connected with the existence of the Jews. . . .
And . . . whatever we do not understand lends itself
only too readily to becoming the target of our contempt
and hatred. In a sense anti-Judaism is the expression of
a fear of spectres.'

Several Gentile contributors, including Dr. Mayer,
single out 'the "chosen people" concept,' or 'irritant,'
as one of the main sources of anti-Judaism. But do not
most nations, in one way or another, claim 'election'?[1]
With the Jews the idea is primarily an expression of the
will to survive as a people, clothed in terms of their
religious tradition; and such deliberate perpetuation by
a dispersed people of its traditional way of life, such
'Judæocentrism,' is undoubtedly a challenge to those
who find the existence of the Jew irritating.

None of the Gentile contributors to this book takes

---

[1] Cf. for instance Gioberti 'Del Primato degli Italiani'; the German idea: 'Am deutschen Wesen, Soll die Welt genesen'; the
Russian idea of themselves as the 'God-bearing nation'; Polish
Messianism ('Poland, the Christ among the Nations'); Kipling's
'Recessional' and the 'White Man's Burden,' etc. The more
unhappy a race the more mystical and extravagant are its claims to
'election.'

conscious note of the original, and the only sensible, basis for Jewish survival: the faith in an ultimate national reintegration through the return to the Land of Israel. Take this away and nothing is left but the self-contradictory, inane flounderings of those intellectual acrobats, the Judæocentric assimilationists, who insist on being both elect and indistinguishable, who deny being a nation and yet desire to preserve their identity, and finish by inventing some religio-ethical missions for 'the Jew in Wonderland.' With this kind of jabber, Dr. Ellis Freeman deals in a sober, polite, but conclusive manner: 'The view of the Jew as a religio-ethical apostle is not quite realistic. However sincerely this may be promoted by the ethical leaders of the nation, and however much it may have entered the habit system of Jewish thinking, the fact is that the representative ordinary Jew does not regard himself in these terms. What he wants is to live satisfactorily, at peace with the world and unmolested by his neighbours, quite without regard to any transcendent mission toward mankind.' And 'since the welfare of the Jew and not a vague ethical mission savouring distinctly of rationalization is the issue, and since the problem is how to raise him at least to the level of the less dispossessed groups of the Western world . . . this improvement must lie away from any such ethnocentric emphasis.'

Dr. Freeman's argument points to complete assimilation as the ultimate solution for the Jewish problem (in its extreme form it reads: 'The most certain way of abolishing anti-Semitism would be to abolish Judaism'). Similar views are stated, or adumbrated, by other Gentile collaborators. They despair of finding any immediate cure for anti-Semitism. 'Indiscriminate attack on every form of existent discrimination,' writes Dr. Talcott

Parsons '. . . is not likely to achieve the actual elimination
of anti-Semitism, but on the contrary to intensify the
reactions it attempts to stop.' 'No immediate and specific
therapy for the problem of anti-Semitism is at hand,'
writes Dr. J. F. Brown. 'The most we can do is to
prevent latent anti-Semitism from becoming overt in
the democracies.' The only way in which anti-Semitism
'may be overcome is by an immediate cultural and final
racial assimilation. Consequently responsible leaders of
both Jewish and Gentile groups should do everything
possible to work toward these aims.' But Dr. Brown
himself admits that while 'cultural assimilation . . . will
have to proceed from the side of the Jews,' anti-Semitism
'cuts down the possibility of attempts from the Jewish
side.' 'Even the so-called assimilated Jew,' writes Dr.
Parsons, 'is not completely a member of the general
community, although he may have severed his connection
with the Jewish community.' Dr. Jessie Bernard points
out that assimilation 'is necessarily a lonely road,' which
each Jew must travel as an individual: for as soon as it
becomes 'a group policy,' the Jews by 'acting co-
operatively . . . preserve their identity in the very effort
to erase it.' (But then how can millions travel along the
same road without forming groups?) And Dr. Kennedy
states, once more with blunt directness, that while in
America 'other nationalities are encouraged and expected
to move rapidly toward assimilation,' even outwardly
assimilated Jews 'are supposed to remain a group apart'
and are 'actively discouraged from mingling freely with
Gentile fellow citizens.' They 'are exhibiting clear signs
of assimilation. Nevertheless, there is no evidence to
indicate that prejudice against them on the part of
Gentiles is markedly decreasing.'

'The Gentile seems to insist,' says Dr. Hertzler, that

the Jew 'remain a Jew.' But next he proceeds to tabulate what the Jews would have to do in order to extinguish anti-Semitism by means of assimilation—he starts seriously and ends in bitter facetiousness:

First of all, the Jew will most likely have to do most of the changing, since he is everywhere an almost negligible minority. . . .

Second, to cease to be a cultural irritant the Jew must be completely assimilated. . . .

Third, he will have to be completely absorbed ethnically. . . .

Fourth, he will have to give up all pride in his group and his people's history. . . .

Fifth, he will have to thrust himself into the background in his economic activities and never allow himself to be numerous or conspicuously successful as a competitor in any occupation, profession, or other economic pursuit. . . .

Finally, he will have to be absolutely sure, generation after generation, while he is gradually disappearing as a Jew, that he does nothing or allows no chance thing to happen that might arouse any of the age-old latent anti-Semitic prejudices or attitudes of non-Jews. . . .

Just to be sure that this does not happen he had better arrange: (1) to ensure the uninterrupted sway of peace and prosperity, for at such times it is easier for men to be brothers, and scapegoats are less necessary; (2) to have all history books burned while he is in process of complete assimilation and amalgamation; (3) if possible, to have all non-Jews develop a case of permanent amnesia.

In this, and other passages, Dr. Hertzler admits the bankruptcy of assimilation as a solution for the Jewish problem; and so do other contributors. But they still hang on to it, for a solution there must be, and they can see no other.

Jews who contribute descriptive articles to this book

admit the strength of the Zionist movement among American Jewry. Dr. Koenig, in his survey of Jewry in Stamford, Conn., states that most of its Jews sympathize with Zionism, 'either actively or passively.' Professor L. Bloom, analysing a Mid-Western centre, says that although its Jews regard Palestine principally 'as another charity,' its development 'lends credence to the idea of nationality.' Dr. Bernard records how even among American Jews 'who had openly proclaimed the doctrine and espoused the policy of assimilation,' the portent of Nazi racial doctrines and persecutions has evoked 'a renewed interest in Zionism, in Hebrew, in religion.' Seeing 'that emancipation is nowhere secure,' Dr. Hertzler admits, seeing that being a decent citizen does not necessarily secure for the Jew decent treatment, that liberal opinion is impotent or passive when persecutions start—the Jew concludes that assimilation 'is one of the greatest myths that he has ever believed.' (Still, Dr. Hertzler asks why in countries where persecutions have not—as yet—broken out, 'young, supposedly assimilated Jews, with their political and economic and social opportunities, want to go to the marshes or deserts of Palestine painfully to try to hew out an eight-acre orange grove?')

In several essays by Gentiles there is an approach to the Zionist idea, though the obvious conclusions are not drawn. Thus Dr. Mayer writes with deep insight into the problem (the italics are his): 'If emancipation has failed, it can be attributed to the fact that *it tried to emancipate the Jews yet did not try to emancipate the Jewish people* . . . emancipation on a purely humanistic individualistic basis is insufficient.' Dr. Stonequist speaks 'a word of caution' against exaggerating the degree to which the Jews in the Diaspora have lost the objective foundations of a national existence: 'It is true that most Jews have not lived in the original homeland, Palestine. But have the Jews as a group ever ceased to regard Palestine as their true homeland? . . . has not Hebrew continued to be the symbol if not the vehicle of continuity of communication?' He further acknowledges that the reintegration of the Jews 'in a sovereign territory of their own' would solve their problem, but dismisses Palestine, because of the smallness of its territory, because of Arab 'needs,' British interests, and the reluctance of 'countless Jews' to go there.

Zionism apparently does not loom large in the eyes of Gentiles who watch the Jewish problem in America: unless there is a further serious deterioration in the position of American Jews, comparatively few are expected to leave the United States for Palestine. Even so, the Jewish future in Palestine deserves closer consideration, for the rise of a Jewish State and Commonwealth in Palestine, or the frustration of Jewish hopes and endeavours, will deeply affect the Jewish problem even in the United States. Gentile contributors emphasize the effect which the 'unique phenomenon' of the Jewish people has on the Gentile mind. Zionism aims at restoring normality to the Jewish people, and a normal national existence in Palestine will radiate normality into the Dispersion. Then the Jews will be raised 'at least to the level of the less dispossessed groups of the Western world,' and will share their further evolution in America.

8

THE JEWISH QUESTION

THE DEVELOPMENTS of the last sixty-five years have made the Jewish question primarily a problem of the English-speaking world, and of this fact the Anglo-American Commission of Inquiry of 1946, was the logical, though perhaps not fully conscious, expression. In 1880 almost 75 per cent of world Jewry inhabited the great Russian-Polish Pale and its fringes; only 3 per cent lived in the United States and 1 per cent in the British Empire, while a powerful agglomeration of Jewish intelligentsia and wealth was growing up in Central Europe: in Berlin, Hamburg, Frankfort, Vienna, etc., with outposts in Prague and Budapest.

Numerically this was the period of the East European Yiddish-speaking masses, culturally and economically of the Central European German-speaking Jew. Between 1880 and 1930 2,500,000 Jews migrated from Eastern Europe to the United States and some 300,000 to Great Britain, Canada, and South Africa; by 1930 only 45 per cent of world Jewry were left in the East European Pale, while 30 per cent had come to inhabit English-speaking countries. With Russian Jewry subdivided or isolated, and generally impoverished by the social, economic, and territorial changes of 1917–20, and German-speaking Jewry weakened by the defeat of the Central Powers, the economic and cultural, and even the numerical, centre was shifting to America.

The advent of the Nazis hastened that process catastrophically. Even before the outbreak of the Second World War Hitler had virtually destroyed Central European Jewry, and during the years 1939–45 the Nazis well-nigh exterminated the Jewish population of most countries under their occupation, from the Pyrenees to the Leningrad-Moscow-Stalingrad line and from Norway to Greece. Of 800,000 Jews in Germany and Austria fewer than 20,000 remain, and of over 2,000,000 in ethnic Poland fewer than 80,000; of over a million in France, Belgium, Holland, Denmark, Norway, Czechoslovakia, Italy, Yugoslavia, Bulgaria, and Greece perhaps one-third; of under a million in the present territories of Hungary and Rumania and of 5,000,000 in the U.S.S.R. possibly half. A certain number have emigrated or escaped to America, Great Britain, Palestine, etc., or continue as 'displaced persons' in Europe. But 6,000,000 Jews have been murdered, and world Jewry has been reduced from about 16,750,000 in 1939 to about 10,750,000 in 1946.

Of these about 5,000,000 now inhabit the United States, 750,000 the British Empire, and 600,000 Palestine; together there are now about six and one-third millions in English-speaking countries or under British administration, forming almost 60 per cent of world Jewry. There are probably about 2,500,000 in Soviet Russia, some 750,000 in the rest of Europe, 500,000 in South America, and 750,000 in the Moslem countries from Morocco to Persia. Of the survivors in Europe, and especially in Central and Eastern Europe, only a fraction wish to remain in their original homes, still less to return to them; the rest desire to emigrate, most of them to Palestine, and much smaller numbers to the United States or the British Empire—apart from other considerations, because in those countries virtually all these would-be migrants have relatives or friends ready to receive them. With the example of Argentina before their eyes, few are likely to be attracted by South America. Soviet Russia is a closed world. From the Moslem countries, infected with rabid Fascist nationalisms, a great many Jews will wish, or will be forced, to migrate; and for most of these Palestine is the natural, and in fact the only possible, refuge.

When the present generation will have passed away hardly any German or Polish speaking Jews will be left, while in the U.S.S.R., Jewry, isolated and dispersed (for the Pale has been liquidated by the Second World War), will decline through intermarriage and assimilation. Half of world Jewry already speaks English, and the time is not far distant when two-thirds will do so—an incomparably higher proportion than ever used a language of the Diaspora as their own: for in the East European Pale most Jews spoke Yiddish, while the German-speaking Jews, though at one time dominant culturally, socially, and economically, never comprised more than one-tenth of the whole.

Thus the fate and future of Jewry is now bound up with that of the English-speaking world—and vice versa. As the immigrants acquire the English language and they and their children rise in the social and cultural scale, their presence makes itself increasingly felt. For no one—least of all the anti-Semites—will call the Jews unimportant or describe them as inconspicuous. There are now almost six times as many Jews in the English-speaking countries as there ever were in those of the German tongue.

What will be the outcome? Agglomerations, more especially of prosperous, educated Jews, after a period of uneasy symbiosis, have so far almost invariably produced catastrophes, and not for the Jews only. The Spain of the Inquisition, Tsarist Russia, and Nazi Germany are the three outstanding cases in modern history, while in Poland, Hungary, and Rumania the anti-Semitic catastrophe had to await Hitler merely because it requires power to give free rein to intense, well-nigh insane hatreds. But once these are unleashed they destroy morally, and even politically, nations possessed by them. In view of past experience, the time seems to have come for the English-speaking nations and their Jewries frankly and seriously to ask themselves the question whether there is a danger of that recurrent catastrophe being reproduced in their countries. Or, to put it inversely, what ground is there for assuming that they alone will be exempt from it? Anti-Semitism is already strong in the United States, Canada, and South Africa, and on the increase in Great Britain (it was kept down by a truly Christian culture which seems to be losing ground). And if there is such a latent danger, what means is there of checking it?

The existence of the Jews in the Dispersion is the source of anti-Semitism—this sounds like a platitude and yet is fraught with meaning. What is it that distinguishes the Jews from all other communities? The mysterious, undefinable bond whereby a remnant has been kept together throughout the ages, throughout the world, whatever their racial type, whatever the colour of their skin, whatever the language they speak, whatever the life they live, often even irrespective of the religion they hold—or do not hold. There has been no other such nation. What is it that binds them together and shapes their destiny? In terms of religion: the will and bidding of God; in terms of politics: a unique, unbreakable obsession of a stiffnecked people. Whichever terms are applied, the ultimate goal as defined in both is the same: the return to Palestine 'that they may live.'

Except for the Return, Jewish survival would be a tragic absurdity—the history of a people which to no purpose, but at the cost of infinite sufferings, has kept out of the great stream of human development, or rather the two streams, which sprang from Judaism: the European stream of Christianity and the Asiatic-African stream of Mohammedanism. While numbers have broken away, a core has remained, and these, gathered round the Ark of the Covenant, have adhered to their national heritage, the Law and the Prophets, and awaited the coming of Messiah and the Return. And to secure the survival of the nation the interpreters of the Law have made it into a wall between the Jew and his neighbour: the first architects of the ghetto.

To the true Jew his destiny is clear and beyond dispute; and so it is to Christians imbued with the teaching of the Old Testament. But it is seldom given to nations or even to men to walk by the light of their faith. Everyday life imposes its compromises on man, and the most discreet of compromises is passivity—to wait for that to happen which it may be incumbent on him to achieve. Inactive survival has for eighteen centuries been the Jewish compromise between faith and reality: a phantom existence in the valley of the dry bones. But the abnormal, incomprehensible half-life of the Jew suggests a double life to his neighbours; it renders him suspect and socially ill-adjusted, and turns him into an irritant and a fit subject for the release of passions born of dark fears and suppressed hatreds.

Of all men, the Jew alone has to account for his presence, and he who can be called upon to justify that, stands condemned before he is judged. If the Jew accepts the challenge and tries to explain, he submits to indignity and flounders into feeble excuses. The most fearless, incisive analysis of his individual existence could merely set forth the compromises or adjustments which he attempts between a destiny that transcends the framework of a man's life and the conditions under which he has to carry on. The ultimate answer to the Jewish Question, that mysterious age-long and world-wide problem, can only be given in the crystal-clear terms of the creed which has created and continued it, in terms of the Jewish nation: survival was the behest and the Return is the purpose.

But there are Jews who assert that Judaism is only a religion, and that they themselves differ from their neighbours merely in that they happen to profess that religion. They strip it of its national content and next of its tradition and ritual—in fact, of practically all distinctive character; and then they expatiate on the supreme 'ethical values' of Judaism—which, though 'universal,' they seem to confine to their own racial community, for they refrain from proselytizing. Not satisfied with disclaiming Jewish nationality for themselves, many of these Judæocentric assimilationists deny it even in others—and that after a Hebrew-speaking Jewish national community has re-arisen in Palestine. But their feverish virulence suggests that it is something within themselves against which they are fighting: indeed, is it not the desire for communal survival which still binds them to their discoloured creed?

There is a native tribe in Ethiopia which claims Jewish descent; about the Sabbath and the Day of Atonement their minds were found to be blank, but hearing the word 'Yerushalayim' (Jerusalem) they eagerly replied,

'That is where we come from.' This memory and hope, with its national content, forms the core of the Jewish religion, and is apt to survive the religion as such. There have been Jews who, though deeply attracted by Christianity, refused baptism in order not to separate from their people—Bergson and Werfel are examples; others who, though baptized, remained outspokenly conscious Jews—for instance, Disraeli and Heine. The charge of 'irreligion' is sometimes levelled against the Zionists by Gentile opponents. But the Jew who works for the Return, and still more the one who effects it, bears the truest testimony to his faith, and it is a spiritual indiscretion in unfriendly strangers to set up as interpreters of the Jewish religion.

Inactive survival perpetuates the ghetto; and the ghetto of the spirit is worse than that of stone walls. There is something both cruel and comforting about a wall: it excludes and protects, is concrete and final; whereas in the airy realms of ideas there is room for self-deception, for clever reinterpretations and false harmonies which break down under pressure. It avails the Jew nothing if he makes a furtive, hesitant bow in the house of Rimmon, or if by the fleshpots of Egypt he weeps for Zion. The countless compromise solutions of the Jewish question are a suppuration of the invisible ghetto, and in the end spell disaster. The ghetto must disappear, the Galuth (Exile) must end. This can be achieved in two ways: through national reintegration in Palestine, and through deliberate dissolution, or ultimate dissolubility, in the Diaspora. The two methods are mutually complementary; both achieve normality and put an end to the Jew of 'the Jewish Question.' The rebuilding of Zion is the fulfilment of God's promise and bidding, or, in terms of unbelief, of the most peculiar and most persistent obsession in history. When this is accomplished, day will break and the guard will be relieved. We shall be a nation, like unto all nations, a nation and not a problem. Then those who have struck roots in other soil will be able to separate with dignity; they are like to the Reubenites, the Gadites, and half the tribe of Manasseh, who, though given lands east of the Jordan, were allowed no rest—'until the Lord have given your brethren rest, as He hath given you, and they also have possessed the land which the Lord your God giveth them.'

In the last fifty years the Jews have entered the two paths of reintegration and dissolution with growing resolve, and both as Zionists and as 'non-Aryan Christians' have met with little understanding and doubtful succour from the Gentiles (and with obstruction from the 'assimilated' Jews). There are anti-Semites who, because opposed to the Jew in the Gentile world, support Zionism—but they are few. Far more common are those who embitter the life of the Jew in the Dispersion and follow him with their hatred to Palestine; who will not let him either live or die in honour; or who, like Hitler and Himmler, when murdering him, decree that he shall die under torture. Besides, there are those, even in most responsible positions, who will not face the Jewish Question in its fatal greatness but treat it with levity; who talk and act as if to the Jew Palestine was just the same as any other land, and who list the National Home among palliatives to be dispensed by them at their own convenience; who try to whittle down the Jewish Question to the problem of the broken remnant in the camps or on the roads of devastated, hostile Europe, and invite those martyred creatures to apply their 'genius' to Europe's reconstruction. They close their eyes to the past, present, and future—even to their own future.

For the core of the Jewish problem is now the 55 per cent of world Jewry resident in English-speaking countries, and the question is whether on that stage too the recurrent Jewish tragedy is to be re-enacted. A Jewish Commonwealth in Palestine within the framework of the British Empire, or possibly of an even wider 'Atlantic Union,' would differentiate the future of the Jews from their past; and now is the time for the Anglo-Saxons to make their decision. But it is incumbent on the Jews of the English-speaking countries to pose the problem unmistakably: if 100,000 young Jews, of American or British birth, came forward and demanded admission to Palestine, national redemption and not individual salvation would be fixed as the goal. But if they and the English-speaking nations shirk the issue, and wait until an acute Jewish Question has arisen in their own countries, they will have waited too long.

9

LEADERSHIP IN ISRAEL: CHAIM WEIZMANN

IF A study were written of leadership among nations in exile or nations in bondage, it would have to start with Joseph and Moses, and would never altogether leave the Jews. The distinguishing mark of the refugee, deportee, or *émigré*—in short, of a 'displaced person'—is that he has not given up the hope or the wish for a return to his native land: the moment he does, he changes into an immigrant. But if such sojourners in strange lands are sufficiently numerous and coherent to form a community of their own, and their stay becomes chronic, leadership among them is divided in character: the authority of the exilarch must rest, in the first place, on the favour or position he enjoys with the host-nation; it may thus be independent of the degree of esteem in which he is held by his own people, or at least that esteem may be of an extraneous, reflected nature. He is the spokesman of his people rather than its leader—Joseph at the court of Pharaoh. On the other hand, even the greatest spiritual leader and paramount judge of a community which lives on sufferance is distinguished by little if any authority beyond its own bounds: he can be a prophet only at home. The political pursuit in which the two forms of authority over a people in exile become reunited is the Exodus—Moses facing Pharaoh. But even he, having to deal with the Jews assimilated at least to the fleshpots, and with the sufferings and murmurings of the crowds in the wilderness, did not find his task an easy one.

Baron Aguilar Pereira, a rich Jew ennobled by Maria Theresa, represents the type of spokesman of the ghetto period. He is said to have supplied the Empress with the money to build Schönbrunn, and thereby to have saved his co-religionaries from expulsion: the new palace of the Empress was the price paid for their being permitted to continue in the ghettos of Vienna, Prague, etc. Whether true or apocryphal, the story sums up centuries of Jewish history: individual Jews acquired large fortunes, and if legal scruples prevented the rulers from seizing their wealth outright (as Edward I did in 1290, Ferdinand and Isabella in 1492, and Hitler in our time), these rich *Schutz- und Hofjuden* (protected Court-Jews) were able to purchase titles and immunity for themselves, and some measure of toleration for their poorer brethren. It was they who represented Jewry in the eyes of a hostile world. The saints and scholars and teachers revered by the Jews, who interpreted to them the Word of God and upheld their courage in suffering and disaster, were hardly known to the Gentiles, still less esteemed by them.

When the Age of Enlightenment brought short-lived respite, 'emancipated' Jews began to emerge from the ghetto and enter the ways of the Gentiles; as scholars, writers, and even as statesmen, a good many of them, in spite of prejudice and handicaps, achieved repute and recognition—but they did so as individuals, not as representatives of their people and its lore: for their ascent in itself necessitated at least a measure of 'assimilation.' Even less fit than the bankers, and in most cases much less willing, were these intellectuals to speak for the Jewish masses.

When the disenchantment of the newly won and very precarious freedom began to break on the Jews, some fifty years ago, there emerged the first 'statesman of the stateless people,' Theodor Herzl. But his was a purely political creed, seeking realization by methods still akin to those of the Pereiras. 'None of us would wish to reject the great idea that Zionism is a political movement,' said in 1907 his follower and critic (and ultimately his successor) Chaim Weizmann. 'But do not reduce politics to a mere approach to Governments and asking their opinion about Zionism.' Herzl was a Central-European Jew, out of touch with the Jewish masses in Eastern Europe: he did not think of them as a potential force, but rather as an object for a new type of Western-Jewish philanthropy. He gave the lead, but 'did not know the workaday reality' which had yet to be faced and tested; this fell to Weizmann, the exponent of 'synthetic Zionism,' a bold programme backed by patient endeavour, and basing its claim on practical achievement.

Weizmann is the first leader in the Dispersion acknowledged as such by the vast majority of Jews throughout the world and officially recognized by the Powers; and for the first time since the destruction of the Temple has a chance of national resurrection and reintegration come to the Jewish people. Weizmann was instrumental in securing it, and has guided the effort to convert it into a reality. But the time of the greatest chance was also that of disasters unparalleled even in Jewish history. Weizmann's path has been grievous—hard almost beyond endurance. His burden has exceeded that of other statesmen: for he has had neither their power nor their resources, nor a clearly defined standing. Lord Balfour, 'a master in the art of politics,' discerned the snag and contradiction. 'Often my uncle would descant to me,' writes Mrs. Edgar Dugdale, 'about the extraordinary difficulties of carrying political responsibility without political power, as the President of the Jewish Agency is compelled to do under the Mandatory régime.'[1] His constituency encircled the globe, but he had no coercive power over his followers, nor any physical force to oppose to their enemies. The perquisites of the responsible statesman were lacking. He was even without power to tax: for his budget he had to rely on voluntary contributions, and a great deal of his time, thought, and energy had to be devoted to the raising of funds. Millions were required for the upbuilding of the National Home: to buy land at fancy prices and reclaim it, to bring in immigrants, to train and re-educate them. He was criticized by some to whom his methods seemed too slow and pedestrian. 'If there is any other way of building up a country,' said Weizmann in 1931, 'save acre by acre, and man by man, and farmstead by farmstead ... I do not know it.' 'The walls of Jericho fell to the sound of shouts and trumpets; I never heard of any walls being raised by such means.'

It was part of the extraordinary interplay of assignment, tragedy, and performance that in the very month of the Balfour Declaration the Bolshevist Revolution cut off from Palestine the Russian Jews, whose strong communal life had engendered a national consciousness in modern Jewry and who supplied the Zionist movement with its best leaders and workmen, and its most generous donors. Financial support had now to be sought mainly in America and Western Europe: and here the feeling among the wealthy was different. To enlist the support of hesitant men with half-avowed sympathies, Weizmann had to include a non-Zionist branch in the enlarged Jewish Agency: it was formed in 1929—and the economic

[1] *Chaim Weizmann. A Tribute on his Seventieth Birthday.* Edited by P. Goodman. Gollancz. 1945.

crisis which supervened falsified once more well-founded expectations. And yet, in spite of many discouragements and obstacles, the National Home was growing. 'I was able to achieve my task through hard and sorrowful work only,' said Weizmann. 'The way does not come to meet you.'

This he said in 1927, when the position of his people seemed more favourable than before or after:

> Our movement . . . has produced the elements of a Jewish Community in Palestine, and it has normalized the attitude of the world towards the Jewish problem. . . .
>
> The Balfour Declaration led to the Mandate and to that stabilization of political conditions which is a pre-condition of our work. . . . It has widely opened the gates for unhampered activity. . . . It has made us masters of our fate . . . politically and socially: what we sow we shall reap. . . .
>
> Still, neither the newly gained understanding of the Jewish problem, nor the will to master once more our destiny as a people, was sufficient to effect the great change, but work, devoted and humble work, in the service of this ideal, this is what has made us a different people. . . . We are right in the middle of productive work. . . . What once seemed a fantastic dream is becoming a historic reality. . . . The Jewish National Home brings together the scattered parts of Jewry on a higher basis of unity than mere reason could provide. . . . Our nationalism means no empty arrogance but a profession of the spiritual and cultural values which are the roots of our existence.

'In the middle of productive work'—this was interrupted two years later by the Arab disturbances of 1929 and the protracted political struggle which followed. 'We were contending not for gains but for rights,' said Weizmann at its close. And he thus defined his attitude ·

We knew that the time for the mass salvation of the Jewish people was not at hand, but we saw in the Balfour Declaration and the Mandate the promise of something much more tangible . . . than what our opponents call 'a spiritual home.' . . . We expected . . . that those among us who greatly desire to go to Palestine, and who feel that there alone they can find peace and satisfaction in creating a national life of their own, would have a reasonable chance of doing so within a reasonable time. We further expected that the material foundations which we should thus have the opportunity of laying would be sufficiently . . . strong safely to bear the superstructure of a moral and intellectual civilization of our own, capable of developing without let or hindrance, repression or suppression. . . .

The Arabs . . . must be convinced . . . that, whatever the future numerical relationship of the two nations in Palestine, we, on our part, contemplate no political domination. But they must also remember that we on our side shall never submit to any political domination. Provided that the Mandate is both recognized and respected, we would welcome an agreement between the two kindred races on the basis of political parity.

There have been repeated readjustments 'of ideas and aims' in Weizmann's programme in order to correlate it 'with the facts of the situation.' When the Palestine Administration and the Royal Commission declared the Mandate unworkable, he accepted the proposal of partitioning Palestine, especially as a Jewish State, even within narrow frontiers, would have meant salvation for the Jews in the days of Nazi persecution—'we are a poor people, ground down and faced with annihilation unless we reintegrate in a National Home.' As he explained at the Zionist Congress of 1937, there are two criteria which he applies in appraising any principle or solution.

The first—does it offer a basis for a genuine growth of Jewish life? I mean both in quality and in volume; does it offer a basis for the development of our young Palestinian culture ... for rearing true men and women, for creating a Jewish agriculture, industry, literature, etc. —in short, all that the ideal of Zionism comprises?

And the other test is:

Does the proposal contribute to the solution of the Jewish problem, a problem pregnant with danger to ourselves and to the world? . . .

I told the Royal Commission that the hopes of 6,000,000 Jews are centred on emigration. Then I was asked: 'But can you bring 6,000,000 to Palestine?' I replied: 'No. I am acquainted with the laws of physics and chemistry, and I know the force of material factors. In our generation I divide the figure by three, and you can see in that the depth of the Jewish tragedy—two millions of youth, with their lives before them, who have lost the most elementary of rights, the right to work.'

The old ones will pass, they will bear their fate or they will not. They are dust, economic and moral dust, in a cruel world. And again I thought of our tradition. What is tradition? It is telescoped memory. We remember . . . the words of Isaiah and Jeremiah. . . . Two millions, and perhaps less; *she'erith hapleta*—only a remnant shall survive. We have to accept it.

The scheme proposed by the Royal Commission, writes Mr. Amery, 'first warmly espoused by the British Government, was allowed to peter out in the shoals and sand of hesitation'; and of the 6,000,000 merely a tiny fraction survived the worst massacre in history.

In 1918, toward the end of the war, Weizmann went to Transjordan, to meet Emir (later King) Feisal. Having

arrived at Lord Allenby's camp, after a long and tiring
journey from Akaba, he washed and changed and then
walked out in the cool of the evening. He was in the land
of Moab, and over there in the west, beyond the Jordan,
he beheld in the fading light the Hills of Judaea and the
hills above Jerusalem. Thus Abraham must have seen
them when he approached the land which God had
promised to His people.

> And there and then two thousand, three thousand,
> four thousand years were effaced. I felt, I knew, it had
> been only yesterday that I had possessed the country; it
> had only been yesterday that our forefather Abraham had
> trodden this ground and set out on the way of his people
> under God's guidance and with His blessing. And then I
> felt all the years of our exile, all the countries we had
> inhabited, all the sufferings we had endured, to be like
> nothing. The gulf had been bridged. This was home;
> this was the promise and the fulfilment; this was certainty.

But next from his dreams and visions Weizmann was
suddenly roused by the voice of a British Tommy
who had come up from behind: 'Sir, you are out of
bounds.'

In dealings with the Mandatory Power, Weizmann,
protected and estopped, supported and frustrated, has
shown loyalty and understanding. He has always remembered the idealism which produced the Balfour Declaration: it had 'its roots in a close study of the Bible,' in the
desire to contribute 'towards the solution of a dread
question which has become a black spot in the life of
mankind'—'the utilitarian motive came last.' Still, disappointment set in early: 'we have not been on a honey-
moon with the Palestine Administration.' And in 1931:
'We have consistently . . . done everything we properly
could to facilitate the task of the Mandatory Power in

Palestine . . . we did not always meet with the response we thought we deserved.'

But it was only at the Zionist Congress of 1937, when threatened by a very severe cutting down of Jewish immigration—contrary to the hitherto accepted regulating principle of 'economic absorptive capacity'—that Weizmann broke out bitterly:

> This is a breach of the promise made to us . . . and the blow is the more cruel because it falls upon us in the hour of our own supreme crisis.
>
> I say this, I who for twenty years have made it my life-work to explain the Jewish people to the British and the British people to the Jews. And I say it to you who have so often attacked me, just because I had taken that task upon myself. . . .
>
> I say to the Mandatory Power: You shall not play fast and loose with the Jewish nation . . . this trifling with a nation bleeding from a thousand wounds must not be done by the British whose Empire is built on moral principles. . . .

And here the story had better stop for the present.

Revised December, 1966

harper ✦ torchbooks

HUMANITIES AND SOCIAL SCIENCES

American Studies: General

American Studies: Colonial

American Studies: From the Revolution to 1860

† The New American Nation Series, edited by Henry Steele Commager and Richard B. Morris.

‡ American Persectives series, edited by Bernard Wishy and William E. Leuchtenburg.

* The Rise of Modern Europe series, edited by William L. Langer.

¶ Researches in the Social, Cultural, and Behavioral Sciences, edited by Benjamin Nelson.

§ The Library of Religion and Culture, edited by Benjamin Nelson.

Σ Harper Modern Science Series, edited by James R. Newman.

○ Not for sale in Canada.

△ Not for sale in the U. K.

FRANCIS J. GRUND: Aristocracy in America: *Social Class in the Formative Years of the New Nation*   TB/1001

ALEXANDER HAMILTON: The Reports of Alexander Hamilton. ‡ *Edited by Jacob E. Cooke*   TB/3060

THOMAS JEFFERSON: Notes on the State of Virginia. ‡ *Edited by Thomas P. Abernethy*   TB/3052

JAMES MADISON: The Forging of American Federalism: *Selected Writings of James Madison. Edited by Saul K. Padover*   TB/1226

BERNARD MAYO: Myths and Men: *Patrick Henry, George Washington, Thomas Jefferson*   TB/1108

JOHN C. MILLER: Alexander Hamilton and the Growth of the New Nation   TB/3057

RICHARD B. MORRIS, Ed.: The Era of the American Revolution   TB/1180

R. B. NYE: The Cultural Life of the New Nation: 1776-1801. † *Illus.*   TB/3026

FRANCIS S. PHILBRICK: The Rise of the West, 1754-1830. † *Illus.*   TB/3067

TIMOTHY L. SMITH: Revivalism and Social Reform: *American Protestantism on the Eve of the Civil War*   TB/1229

FRANK THISTLETHWAITE: America and the Atlantic Community: *Anglo-American Aspects, 1790-1850* TB/1107

ALBION W. TOURGÉE: A Fool's Errand. ‡ *Ed. by George Fredrickson*   TB/3074

A. F. TYLER: Freedom's Ferment: *Phases of American Social History from the Revolution to the Outbreak of the Civil War. 31 illus.*   TB/1074

GLYNDON G. VAN DEUSEN: The Jacksonian Era: 1828-1848. † *Illus.*   TB/3028

LOUIS B. WRIGHT: Culture on the Moving Frontier   TB/1053

American Studies: The Civil War to 1900

THOMAS C. COCHRAN & WILLIAM MILLER: The Age of Enterprise: *A Social History of Industrial America* TB/1054

W. A. DUNNING: Essays on the Civil War and Reconstruction. *Introduction by David Donald*   TB/1181

W. A. DUNNING: Reconstruction, Political and Economic: 1865-1877   TB/1073

HAROLD U. FAULKNER: Politics, Reform and Expansion: 1890-1900. † *Illus.*   TB/3020

HELEN HUNT JACKSON: A Century of Dishonor: *The Early Crusade for Indian Reform. ‡ Edited by Andrew F. Rolle*   TB/3063

ALBERT D. KIRWAN: Revolt of the Rednecks: *Mississippi Politics, 1876-1925*   TB/1199

ROBERT GREEN MC CLOSKEY: American Conservatism in the Age of Enterprise: 1865-1910   TB/1137

ARTHUR MANN: Yankee Reformers in the Urban Age: *Social Reform in Boston, 1880-1900*   TB/1247

WHITELAW REID: After the War: *A Tour of the Southern States, 1865-1866. ‡ Edited by C. Vann Woodward*   TB/3066

CHARLES H. SHINN: Mining Camps: *A Study in American Frontier Government. ‡ Edited by Rodman W. Paul*   TB/3062

VERNON LANE WHARTON: The Negro in Mississippi: 1865-1890   TB/1178

American Studies: 1900 to the Present

RAY STANNARD BAKER: Following the Color Line: *American Negro Citizenship in Progressive Era. ‡ Edited by Dewey W. Grantham, Jr.*   TB/3053

RANDOLPH S. BOURNE: War and the Intellectuals: *Collected Essays, 1915-1919. ‡ Edited by Carl Resek*   TB/3043

A. RUSSELL BUCHANAN: The United States and World War II. † *Illus.*   Vol. I TB/3044; Vol. II TB/3045

ABRAHAM CAHAN: The Rise of David Levinsky: *a documentary novel of social mobility in early twentieth century America. Intro. by John Higham*   TB/1028

THOMAS C. COCHRAN: The American Business System: *A Historical Perspective, 1900-1955*   TB/1080

FOSTER RHEA DULLES: America's Rise to World Power: 1898-1954. † *Illus.*   TB/3021

JOHN D. HICKS: Republican Ascendancy: 1921-1933. † *Illus.*   TB/3041

SIDNEY HOOK: Reason, Social Myths, and Democracy   TB/1237

ROBERT HUNTER: Poverty: *Social Conscience in the Progressive Era. ‡ Edited by Peter d'A. Jones*   TB/3065

WILLIAM L. LANGER & S. EVERETT GLEASON: The Challenge to Isolation: *The World Crisis of 1937-1940 and American Foreign Policy*   Vol. I TB/3054; Vol. II TB/3055

WILLIAM E. LEUCHTENBURG: Franklin D. Roosevelt and the New Deal: 1932-1940. † *Illus.*   TB/3025

ARTHUR S. LINK: Woodrow Wilson and the Progressive Era: 1910-1917. † *Illus.*   TB/3023

GEORGE E. MOWRY: The Era of Theodore Roosevelt and the Birth of Modern America: 1900-1912. † *Illus.*   TB/3022

RUSSEL B. NYE: Midwestern Progressive Politics: *A Historical Study of Its Origins and Development, 1870-1958*   TB/1202

WILLIAM PRESTON, JR.: Aliens and Dissenters: *Federal Suppression of Radicals, 1903-1933*   TB/1287

WALTER RAUSCHENBUSCH: Christianity and the Social Crisis. ‡ *Edited by Robert D. Cross*   TB/3059

JACOB RIIS: The Making of an American. ‡ *Edited by Roy Lubove*   TB/3070

PHILIP SELZNICK: TVA and the Grass Roots: *A Study in the Sociology of Formal Organization*   TB/1230

IDA M. TARBELL: The History of the Standard Oil Company: *Briefer Version. ‡ Edited by David M. Chalmers*   TB/3071

GEORGE B. TINDALL, Ed.: A Populist Reader ‡   TB/3069

TWELVE SOUTHERNERS: I'll Take My Stand: *The South and the Agrarian Tradition. Intro. by Louis D. Rubin, Jr., Biographical Essays by Virginia Rock*   TB/1072

WALTER E. WEYL: The New Democracy: *An Essay on Certain Political Tendencies in the United States. ‡ Edited by Charles B. Forcey*   TB/3042

Anthropology

JACQUES BARZUN: Race: *A Study in Superstition. Revised Edition*   TB/1172

JOSEPH B. CASAGRANDE, Ed.: In the Company of Man: *Twenty Portraits of Anthropological Informants. Illus.*   TB/3047

W. E. LE GROS CLARK: The Antecedents of Man: *Intro. to Evolution of the Primates.* º △ *Illus.*   TB/559

CORA DU BOIS: The People of Alor. *New Preface by the author. Illus.*   Vol. I TB/1042; Vol. II TB/1043

RAYMOND FIRTH, Ed.: Man and Culture: *An Evaluation of the Work of Bronislaw Malinowski* ¶ º △   TB/1133

DAVID LANDY: Tropical Childhood: *Cultural Transmission and Learning in a Puerto Rican Village* ¶   TB/1235

L. S. B. LEAKEY: Adam's Ancestors: *The Evolution of Man and His Culture. △ Illus.*   TB/1019

ROBERT H. LOWIE: Primitive Society. *Introduction by Fred Eggan*   TB/1056

EDWARD BURNETT TYLOR: The Origins of Culture. *Part I of "Primitive Culture." § Intro. by Paul Radin*   TB/33

EDWARD BURNETT TYLOR: Religion in Primitive Culture. *Part II of "Primitive Culture." § Intro. by Paul Radin*   TB/34

W. LLOYD WARNER: A Black Civilization: *A Study of an Australian Tribe.* ¶ *Illus.*   TB/3056

Art and Art History

WALTER LOWRIE: Art in the Early Church. *Revised Edition. 452 illus.*   TB/124

EMILE MÂLE: The Gothic Image: *Religious Art in France of the Thirteenth Century.* § △ *190 illus.*   TB/44

3

History: Renaissance & Reformation

History: Modern European

Intellectual History & History of Ideas

6

Political Science & Government

Psychology

Christianity: General

Christianity: Origins & Early Development

Christianity: The Middle Ages and The Reformation

Christianity: The Protestant Tradition